How To Get
Your Wife In Bed

HOW TO GET
Your Wife
IN Bed

A Practical Plan to Creating a
Powerful Relationship that Lasts a Lifetime

J.S. PETERS

New York

How To Get Your Wife In Bed
A Practical Plan To Creating A Powerful Relationship That Lasts a Lifetime

Cover Design by Johnson2Design: www.Johnson2Design.com
megan@johnson2Design.com

ISBN 978-1-60037-681-8

Library of Congress Control Number: 2009932350

MORGAN · JAMES
THE ENTREPRENEURIAL PUBLISHER

Morgan James Publishing, LLC
1225 Franklin Ave., STE 325
Garden City, NY 11530-1693
Toll Free 800-485-4943
www.MorganJamesPublishing.com

In an effort to support local communities, raise awareness and funds, Morgan James Publishing donates one percent of all book sales for the life of each book to Habitat for Humanity. Get involved today, visit www.HelpHabitatForHumanity.org.

This book has been created to help every man understand what <u>must</u> be done to have the most incredible and valuable relationships of his life: First and foremost with his chosen partner, and then ultimately with everyone in his life.

WARNING

To all the radiant women of the world:
DO NOT READ THIS BOOK.

It was not designed for you but for your benefit. I want to help men become truly great at being in the relationships that they have already chosen. As men, we often struggle asking for help with anything, from asking for driving directions to rekindling a romance. This book is for men, maybe for your man. If he finds something of value, then it has to be, in his way and by his choice.

The worst thing that could happen is for you to read this book and have new expectations of your man that he may (or may not) follow through with. These ideas shouldn't put space between you and your partner. My passion is to teach him how to bring you closer together.

So this book should remain a mystery to you. Allow your man to be incredible in his unique way. Allow him to improve at his speed. Be grateful that he is interested in becoming a better man for you.

You may give this book to a man that you love and respect, adding to his collection of resources. Perhaps, a copy of this book may end up in the hands of YOUR man from someone other than you.

Thank you for your understanding and having patience with all of us men as we continually strive to be better.

To the incredible men reading this book:

I have faith that there are ways for all of us to grow in our relationships. Thank you for sharing this faith. I don't claim to know everything about women. I have had many experiences, talked to many people and collected many ideas to present to you about how to re-create the magic in your love life.

Before you begin this journey with me, here are a few warnings.

Not all women will respond the same to all acts of courtship and dating

You may try certain ideas thinking they will perfectly woo your woman. But, for some reason, they might go over like a ton of bricks. If you follow all of the steps in this book about becoming a whiz at creating dates, you will have a full bag of tricks to overcome these rare occasions. Women can be unpredictable at the best of times. It's the nature of the animal. It's what draws us to them, and if we are honest with ourselves, we all love the challenge of winning our woman's heart. At the end of the day, aren't you glad your woman isn't just 'vanilla' plain and that she has some fire?

A little knowledge can be a dangerous thing

Please have the patience and drive to follow through with reading this ENTIRE book. I understand that you may not be a super romantic guy, and that you may read some of the stuff with disbelief... but keep reading. You will need to have a complete plan before you start to execute.

If you gain just one idea from this book that helps you to strengthen your relationship it will have been worth it. There are several very important principles in this book. After you have finished reading this book, apply them to your love life and start creating romance in your life. These principles will allow you to maintain your personal flavor and style as you ravage the heart of your soul mate.

Just reading this book shows you have the courage to search for ways to continually invest in your intimate relationship.

After reading and acting on this information you will get everything you want from your relationship, I promise. It will be easy to be friends again, you and your goddess will have fun with each other every day and you will have intimacy that will fuel your deepest desires and propel you to anywhere you wish to go in your life.

Let's start the journey.

Table of Contents

Chapter One:

Stopping the War with Kisses

"Never give up, for that is just the place
and time that the tide will turn."

- Harriet Beecher Stowe

Would you like it if when you got home at the end of the day and the love of your life greeted you at the door wearing nothing more than a plaid miniskirt and a corset? Or when you take your lover on a date and then go home, you don't come out of the garage for 30 minutes because she won't stop showering you with affection? Would you like to look at your angel and see her as you did when you first met her; as a perfect 10 that satisfies your every dream and sexual whim?

Does this all seem a little shallow? Maybe

Is it truly what we want in our perfect fantasy world? Yes

Is this all that we want from our relationships? Definitely not

Let's look at a few more questions. Why are so many men using chemical stimulus like Viagra and antidepressants to improve their state of mind and increase sexual prowess in marriages and long-term relationships? Why is the current divorce rate in North America now officially over 50%? The average failed marriage doesn't even last seven years. The divorce rate is going up all around the world. This is completely outrageous. It isn't only our fault, but it is our choice. Would you rather become a part of the statistic or a man of your word? If you are married then you have made an oath to your wife. A man is only worth his word. If we want to drastically decrease this number and not become another statistic, we need to create an abundant relationship that will last our lifetime.

This book will reveal a simple plan to ensure that you are not a part of this statistic. As men we have the ability to reinvest in our relationships to achieve our desired goal of getting our wives back in bed and rebuilding the intimacy. Intimacy is one of the initial building blocks of a relationship and needs to continually grow as part of a strong foundation. Of course there are many other important reasons why we are in relationships and marriages, but at the end of the day, if you have a healthy sex life with your partner, chances are the rest of your relationship is on track.

Sometimes we better understand how relationships between men and women work by looking at other cultures. If we look at shamanic teachings, there are some interesting philosophies. Men are attracted to beauty. Women are attracted to power. It is said that men energize women through their sexual chakra and that women energize men through their heart chakra.

In relationships, when we have disagreements and our feelings get hurt, we often punish each other by preventing each other getting into this chakra. Women shut down intimately and sexually and then don't allow their man to energize them. Men shut down and don't allow their woman to touch their hearts. After several disagreements and some much-earned trust issues and the toilet seat being left up again, both the connection and the relationship start to deteriorate. We often aren't even aware of it until the problem is larger than we can deal with.

Let's look at a real-life example and you'll understand all this chakra stuff a little better. The stereotypical argument would have two unhappy people trying to prove opposite sides of a point. We may raise our voice, not look at each other, physically get hot and excited, say what is on our mind without filtering it and not, under any circumstance, have any intimate physical contact. That is what blocking your chakras looks like. Now what would happen if when you were at the height of passionately bashing each other with words, you somehow could shift that energy and passionately start kissing her. It would happen just like it does in the movies, the lights go low, the Kenny G music starts playing in background and you stop the war with kisses instead of throwing daggers at her heart.

The kissing would lead to other things and your energy is completely transformed, then exchanged with each other and then exhausted. This is having your chakras completely open to one another. You may have experienced the aftershock glow that comes from making love with your lover. That is known in the shamanic teachings as opening up your partner and fully charging her with your sexual charka. By the time you are done your little tryst, whatever problem you were so set on being *right* about, somehow has just vanished or was at least reduced to a size that it is easily resolved. If you haven't tried this technique yet, you need to and at the end of this chapter, I'll show you how. If you have done this by accident or perhaps on purpose, I am sure you can recall the effects of the passion being redirected.

It boils down to this: when a man pursues a woman with great vigour and diligence, showing his complete appreciation for her femininity, it results in trust and emotional intimacy from the woman, which culminates when he chooses her as a mate sexually. Making love to her and being intimate are his gestures of appreciation and love. The woman, in return, gives completely to the man with all of her soul. She is nurturing and takes care of him, physically, emotionally and mentally. She will give all of her being to satisfy her partner's and her family's needs. It is the outpouring of love that a man craves from his woman. It is true nurturing.

It's quite the deal. All we have to do is consciously choose her everyday and ensure she feels appreciated and in return we get unbridled love, sexual intimacy, and compassion. Let me tell you men, we've got the right end of this deal and yet we still find ways to screw it up.

Sadly, we've become a society of instant-gratification seeking, weak-willed men. We have forgotten the rewards that exist when we choose growth. Most people are content with being mediocre in their personal lives and forget to live passionate lives.

We want it all and we want it right now.

We aren't concerned with the distant future. We spend money and time like there's no tomorrow and we're organized if we plan for events next week. We don't plan for what our future will be in 20 years.

These patterns are consistent in many areas of our lives and relationships are no exception.

I say this because I lived this way for a long time. I fell victim to the *instant life*. I jumped from relationship to relationship looking for the next best thing, instead of trusting my ability to both *choose* and *attract* the woman of my dreams.

Realizing that I was unable to trust myself was a huge eye opener. I changed my actions and retrained my brain to be trustworthy. Finally, I could show a woman that I was worthy of her love.

This book will issue challenges. Each challenge is a small task that you can complete quickly. Do each one to propel you towards your dream of an ultimate relationship as well as reconditioning the trust that you have in yourself. These challenges have deadlines. You should take action immediately to achieve the goals.

CHALLENGE ONE

Fill in this statement with your name and today's date.

I, _____, on the ____ day of _____ 20__, commit to reading this book entirely. I will give 100% of my effort to accomplish the challenges and attacking the action plans. I will not let myself down. As a man, I can accomplish anything I put my mind to.

Read the statement aloud and make the commitment to yourself or whoever you answer to. If you cannot do this little task with 100% commitment then you probably shouldn't read this book. Every man has it in himself to accomplish anything he desires. You opened this book because you wanted to learn something, take the first step now.

You want the information in this book and this first challenge is the first step you need to take. Create a plan to set aside the time you need to read this entire book. I would encourage you to set a goal that will finish this book in the next seven days. Take out your day planner or a calendar and physically write down the days and times you will read this book and for how long. The book has been kept relatively short so this goal is achievable for everyone. It is better to attack the book quickly. If you start this adventure and require more time to complete your goal, you will have it, and if you finish all tasks early, you will have free time. Prove to yourself that you can make a plan and stick to it. This first exercise will mirror the results you are going to get from this book and most likely mirror the way you do anything in life. I believe in you. You can create any future you want.

> "Do, or do not. There is no 'try'."
> - Yoda ('The Empire Strikes Back')

Professionally, I have been a golf pro, a ski/snowboarding instructor, a hockey coach, an entrepreneur, a restaurateur, a corporate trainer, a camp director, a youth facilitator/counsellor and a bartender (modern day psychologist).

Even after teaching and working with so many people and understanding how to get the best out of the people I coached, I needed to learn how to be successful in long-term relationships. I needed to become great in this area if I was going to get success in all areas of my life.

I have been married and divorced. I have lived with more women that I should admit to. I have failed in relationships. I tried to justify every past relationship. All my excuses were a big pile of steaming crap. The simple truth I didn't understand was that *I need to continue to win the heart of my woman every day.*

Without investing in her heart, I became complacent, bored and eventually left the relationship in frustration. I read lots of relationship books and, to be honest, they were so complex and out of my comfort zone that I was reluctant to use their ideas.

There is a ton of amazing information out there, which if decoded properly, might be very effective. But not for me and maybe not for you either. I needed something that was easy to understand and follow.

I interviewed many women to get insight into what they really want. I listened to each word and asked for more details when I was confused. I asked questions to find simple solutions that make sense to both sexes.

This relationship building really doesn't need to be mundane or complex. We get into relationships full of excitement and joy. It makes sense that we should be able to maintain that first excitement and joy while seeing continual growth and strengthening of the relationship.

We need to keep doing some of the same things that allowed love to grow when we first fell for our sweetheart. This isn't rocket science; it's simply **dating** and **courtship**. Now, before you decide you'd rather go clean the garage than think about courtship let's look at the **rewards**.

Learning (or re-learning), practicing and mastering these skills will bring your relationship back to the place of passion and fire while giving you the tools to stay there forever. What other areas of your life will be affected when your relationship is running at top speed with passion and fulfilment?

This book will have a massive effect on all areas of your life. Understand that you *need* to read this book and do the challenges to *create* the relationship of your dreams. This strong foundation will become your launching pad for life success. If you don't change your habits, will your results differ?

Commit to reading this book quickly and putting the ideas into practice. It is my firm belief that **dating** and **courtship** allows many key things to happen in a relationship. It creates quality time together; it allows a woman to be relaxed in her feminine way and you get to use your masculine energy.

This difference creates polarity. **Polarity** is what drives men and woman to go crazy over one another. We will go into this in greater detail, but it has to do with balancing each others' 'charge' so you may find true happiness and rediscover the pleasure you had at the beginning of your relationship.

We should all strive to keep those ecstatic feelings in all our relationships. Imagine being in a passionate partnership with the woman of your dreams. How will your intensity affect your career, your relationships with friends and family and your health? Remember when you first fell in love? Everything feels better when you live passionately. To achieve this, all you need to do is continually date and court the woman who won your heart.

Let's keep it simple. Have fun reading this book, let it bring joy back into yours and your partner's life. By bringing joy to your partner, she can give it back to you. Soon you'll find yourselves back in bed....

Instructions - How to stop the war with kisses.

Next time you get in a heated exchange with your true love, here is what you need to do:

1. Breathe deeply. The kind of inhalation that starts at your head and goes all the way into your balls.

2. Next take your over-charged lady in your arms and look right into her eyes.

3. Keep breathing and, still looking deep into her in her eyes, lean in and kiss her lips softly and only for a few short seconds.

4. Move your head back to where you can refocus your gaze on her and tell her that you love her and that you choose to love her forever.

5. Kiss her again.

6. Repeat steps 3 to 5 until she kisses you back.

7. Do whatever feels natural from this point while continuing to breathe deeply and make eye contact as much as possible.

8. Feel both of your hearts opening to their fullest and relish in the experience.

Chapter Two:

Our Reality is Our Choice

Looking back at the romantic relationships in my life, I noticed I had a track record of being very good at the first three to four months of all new relationships. This is the time when everything seems fresh and new and exciting. When I analyzed my successes, I found a few simple yet consistent components. The ability to create magic in the form of dating and courtship led to victory. Consistent effort and attention allowed us to form memories and grow together, heightening our sexual energy exchange and awareness of each other's wants and needs.

The intent of any date is to create a situation where romance and trust can grow. Just taking the steps to arrange quality time with your partner is romantic. The fact that you want to be fully present with your partner and remove all of life's other distractions is romantic. These connected times expand the emotional love, physical love and intellectual love between you and your wife.

It never ceases to amaze me all the effort that we as men will go through to impress a woman. Creating unique and memorable dates is the key to triumph in your relationship. Setting up a drive-in movie theatre in your backyard, cooking a gourmet dinner with a candlelit table, or arranging tickets to the ballet isn't the 'magic', it's the fact that you made these efforts. The response from a great date is always amazing. When you feed a woman's heart, her beauty grows. It is part of how love grows. You both transform through each other's presence and passion. It took me a long time to recognize my pattern of slacking off once I was confident that I had won my woman's heart. I would stop making grand efforts to win her favor. Movie nights were about going to the video store together and picking up something then watching them in oversized workout clothes that could double as pyjamas. Neither of us felt very sexy. Dinner nights often became 'order-in' nights and we would sit on the couch and watch television. We were together in location, but there had been a definite shift in our relationship. It was a recipe for disaster.

I had no idea how to maintain the level of passion that existed at the beginning of my relationships. In a short period of time, usually it could be measured in seasons, I knew I still loved my partner but I was no longer in love with her.

Can you relate to the feeling of being a lacklustre lover? Feeling in love should be hot, and steamy and all-consuming. INFATUATION!!!

Yes, this is possible to find again with your wife. Don't you want back that feeling of simply not being able to get enough of one woman? Being willing to do whatever needs to be done as long as you can be with her. You know exactly what I'm talking about. It's a human emotion and we've all had this feeling at some point. Those times when you would miss your favorite sporting event and go and see some romantic comedy at the theatre, or drive clear across town to meet for a 15-minute lunch break, or have a surprise hotel night booked in your hometown on a Tuesday night, these are all the creative and brilliant ideas you cook up when you are truly in love.

As men, we want to conquer our desires. How do we do this while remaining faithful to one special woman? We are all amazing creators when we want to be. When we desire something in our lives, it often appears.

Be careful what you wish for. If you are wishing for a highly charged and passionate relationship, the universe may simply supply you with another young lady to start over with, after all new is always easier. But is it really better? If you ask for your current relationship to become supercharged with love and passion, I am sure you will get a very different result. Perhaps you can relate to the past cycles of my life. I would be in a relationship that was starting to feel stale and all of a sudden a beautiful new girl would pop into my life. I would hit it off with the new woman and would start the pattern of bye-bye old girlfriend and hello "Miss New." I would feel on fire again and would be able to access all of my creativity and masculine power.

At the time, I didn't know there was another way to create the excitement beyond starting a new relationship with a different person. TV shows and movies rarely show us the rewards of a committed and growing relationship. We usually see how wonderfully romantic affairs can be or how to get away with an affair. We see fairytale romances of wives that have the dinner on the table at 6pm every night. Life just isn't this way and the idea of having a pure and engaging relationship should be your true goal. It would be very refreshing to have a real look at what is required as a man to truly have it all.

Before I understood this, I met a woman who I thought was The One. I thought I had broken my cycle and we got married. I was a committed husband and would never cheat on my wife, but after three years, the passion was long gone. I didn't know how to get it back. I met a beautiful woman at work. She was saving herself for her wedding night and had a boyfriend. I was sure my new friend would fill my need for excitement and fun without any physical strings attached.

I found myself emailing this woman at all hours sharing intimate details of my life. I told her the truth, I was unhappy in my marriage. We would talk about *our* dreams and *our* goals and *our* future. I was planning another life with a new partner before I had left my current one.

If it was just a sexual relationship, my marriage may have lasted. I was giving her all the emotional energy that I should have been giving my wife. It was an emotional affair and I convinced myself that I was doing nothing wrong. So I got divorced. I'm a part of that statistic and I am not proud of this.

You'd be wise to ask yourself what a divorced man can teach you about marriage. Michael Jordan understands perfectly how failure leads to true knowledge and ultimately success. He said, **"I've missed more than 9,000 shots in my career. I've lost almost 300 games. 26 times I've been trusted to take the game-winning shot and missed. I've failed over and over and over again in my life and that is why I succeed."**

Understanding failure is what truly creates expertise. A man who only knows success hasn't learned anything other than

how to use his current knowledge. A man who has taken time to learn from his failure has knowledge we can all learn from.

As men, it can take us a long time to realize that we aren't going to be naturally great at everything we do, including building lasting relationships. Some things come very easy, some things we want to be great at and are willing to work towards and there are some things that we just don't have a talent for.

We bring experts into our life to take care of things we don't have a talent for. An accountant does the taxes for my businesses. A mechanic at the Honda dealership replaces the brakes on my car. And my tailor, Danny, makes all of my clothes actually fit my body. I could learn to do all of these things, but there are some things that aren't worth my time or energy.

When there is something that I really do want to learn, I gather a team of coaches, professional or otherwise. When I was a golf pro I had a team that consisted of a swing coach, a physical trainer, a sports psychologist, and a friend to practice with.

With expert guidance and consistent practice, I achieved my goal of scoring par in two years, as opposed to the lifetime struggle that most amateur golfers take to attempt to achieve the same goal. When I started, I could shoot rounds in the 90s. Anything is achievable.

Like many amateur golfers, I believed that if I practiced enough eventually I would get better. But I soon came to learned that if I kept practicing my *current* habits, I wasn't going to improve. Whatever knowledge I had was not all of the knowledge I required to become a professional. Once I found coaches to help me think in new ways, my growth was exponential. The time that it took to achieve my goals was greatly reduced because my practice time had meaning and was measurable and focused. I was no longer wandering aimlessly.

When we desire something and seek the expertise to attain it, everything is possible. When I wanted to become better at building a relationship that would last, I sought out some incredible information from books, psychologists, women and men, both in and out of relationships. I even spoke with my former partners.

We all have the ability to be in relationships; we just need to understand a few more things to become *great* in relationships.

When you are focused on the object of your desire, you are unstoppable.

CHALLENGE 2

I want you to write down three examples of great achievements so far in your lifetime; times when you simply focused on a goal then took massive action and achieved that goal. First write down the achievement and then write down the action steps that you took to achieve the goal.

Accomplishment	Action Steps
1. _____	a. _____
	b _____
	c. _____
2. _____	a. _____
	b. _____
	c. _____
3. _____	a. _____
	b. _____
	c. _____

Do this as a reminder to yourself of the greatness that lives in you. It's easy in our day-to-day lives to forget that we are all capable of creating our destiny. Your destiny is shaped when you have a clear vision of your purpose, then create and follow your plan to its fullest.

Chapter Three:

Ante Up

"If you do not create your **destiny**, you
will have your fate inflicted upon you"

-William Irvin Thompson

It's time to put your money in and play the game of life to its fullest. Are you just sitting around and watching your life go by. Why? The outcome of our efforts, our destiny, is a choice that all men get to make. You lose your right to choose when you stand idly by and have to accept whatever falls in your lap. Choose to create your life and learn that you have the power and ability to create any reality you desire. The success of your love life is completely within your control. As men, we either choose to invest in relationships that grow and flourish, or do nothing and watch them wither away. What are you going to choose?

Why do you want to be in a relationship? I heard it best described like this, "We all just simply want someone to share in all of our memories and lay witness to the achievements in life."

Granted there are many other benefits of being in relationship including having a family, having passionate sex, feeling loved, having someone to cook with, having someone to live with, reducing cost of living and all of that stuff. But when you really break it all down, we don't want to live our lives alone and we want someone who evokes passion in us. As cliché as it may sound, the truth is, "Behind every great man is a great woman." Or at least a woman that helps to feed his passion.

When we look at how most of our time is spent on a daily basis, it revolves around our work, our kids or our parents, our friends and our chosen partner. The way that we prioritize these focuses is usually in this order as well, with work being the number-one time thief and our intimate relationship coming in last.

Looking at the areas of life we tend to remember the most, it is often the time with friends. I don't have many *great* memories of being at a job. In my research, I wasn't surprised to find that most people don't have many *great* memories of their day-to-day work lives, family life or even intimate life.

Friends often hold the highest *great* memory count as we always plan events with them. We are, in essence, continuously planning great dates for our friends and forgetting about everyone else. Sure once or twice a year we plan vacations with our family and yes, memories are created. Can we make our day-to-day life worth remembering?

Being a man that can plan amazing dates gives you the power of generating the opportunity for you and your partner to create incredible *great* memories together whenever you chose. In fact, if you talk to women who've been in long-term relationships and ask them how they know that their man loves them, you will see a pattern. They will often list off very specific individual events or memories that they have of something that their man did in the past that was so noteworthy that they will never forget. We'll call these moments *Shining Man Moments*. They are moments in time that were far enough outside of the norm they deserve to be remembered. They are the moments that get described via texts and emails to all of her friends as soon as she has a free minute after the date. When all of her friends tell her how sweet you are, your stock value goes up in her eyes. When these moments are delivered with passion and love for your woman or your family, there is a strong emotional attachment that will feed the heart of your partner for years to come. I will explain this in greater detail later in the book, as we look at planning grand dates and growing the love for and with your woman.

Aside from the great trips and adventures with your friends you need to create unique memories with the important people in your life. Once, I remember ruining a risotto, but making a great connection, one that has lasted 20 years. I invited a special lady over for a gourmet meal. I was still in school at the time and at 3pm rushed to the market to get some fresh prawns then made a succulent risotto and an incredible dessert from scratch. It took me almost three hours to get everything ready. Dinner was at seven o'clock. She didn't turn up until after 10 o'clock that night. She felt horrible that I had gone to such effort and she was so late.

I didn't get upset and by keeping the mood light, we had an amazing time. To this day, she still talks about *The Dinner* I made her almost 20 years ago. By making an effort to show this woman how much I appreciated her, our relationship flourished and the incident is forever recorded in the record of our time together. Far from romantic, this amazing woman is my mother. I have planned special *dates* with her and other members of my family and have found that our friendship has grown due to creating a unique time and space. This in turn has formed great memories.

I know many couples in long-term relationships who can tell you what their favorite TV shows are for every night of the week. They can list the movies they've seen together. But ask them what their partner was wearing yesterday and often they are sadly challenged. Or ask them the last time they had sex and they need a calendar to jog their memories. Ask them when was the last time they showed each other how much they love each other and what was done to creatively display this. Often it has been far too long to recall at all.

HINT: *If it wasn't in the past 10 days, it was toooooo long ago.... This catastrophic truth explains how we forget what made our relationship foundation strong. What happened to midnight massages, the notes left on the pillow, the little wrapped gifts, the planned dates, the pressed dress shirts and cute little dresses that lead to crazy hot sex?*

If you want an incredibly successful relationship, it takes focused and committed practice and effort to get there.

In the business world, success is often found by creating a system that generates massive cash flow. If you were skilled and/ or lucky enough to create a plan that makes a million dollars in a year, then you can expect similar results the next year if you repeat your plan. It would require the same amount of effort and time as well as the passion to succeed. Have the foresight to modify your plan, if needs be, as times change. But only modify, do NOT scrap the entire model. On the flip side, if you cease to follow that plan and no longer put forth any efforts, you must expect that over time, the money you earned will all be gone and you will be left with nothing. Your millions will have all been spent and you will be broke again. How does this mirror the relationships in your life, or maybe past relationships? Hmmmm....

What's your plan to create and maintain love and passion in your live? If you are married or in a committed relationship, you must have had a successful plan in the beginning of your relationship and you can again.

Dating and courtship are partly the answers. The other part is being an incredible, purposeful man. What is it exactly about dating and courting a woman that is so effective that it allows us to fall in love with one another indefinitely?

Simply explained, courting allows men and women to create attraction and polarity. Polarity is the attraction between a positive and negative charge. Imagine playing with two little magnets and moving them simply by using the charge they make when they *sense* each other.

When men and women are using their masculine and feminine energy in relationships, they are madly attracted to each other. The masculine energy is typically the driving straight line force in life. The feminine energy is considered to be the flowing force that is the creator of life.

I'm not talking about archaic restrictive models of women being barefoot and pregnant in the kitchen and men being the bread winners. What I'm talking about is the energy that we embody in the world. I can give you an example of what we typically recognize as polarity: when a man walks up to a woman and just plants a full on kiss on her lips and you see her go weak at the knees. It is simple to see the arc of polarity, and how it works. The man feels strongly on purpose, alive, vibrant to the core, we can only imagine what the woman feels, but we've all seen her come back to her man and his power. There is a definite direction as to the intent of the man and we would expect to see some sort of further development in a relationship.

The woman's energy is in flow and consumed by the passion. Her response is what allows love to grow between the two. Now, if a woman just plants a kiss on a man, something very strange happens. Surely they will both enjoy the moment. But after the kiss, often they both are a little confused as what to do next. Who is leading, where does this go? There always has to be a leader and a follower, a masculine and a feminine, the positive and the negative charges. If both people are in the *masculine* leading energy, this action seems to go against the natural order and flow of things as neither one knows who to follow and both end up trying to lead.

For a relationship to be effective, one person must take the lead. It doesn't really matter which partner takes which energy as long as you are at opposite ends of the spectrum with your partner. Dating and courtship create the opportunity for you to play within the energetic field. As a man, if you are planning and executing most of your meetings together, that is indeed strong direction.

Through these dates, a woman will flow and play; creating and growing a bond between the two of you. Before you know it, Cupid will have flung his arrow straight into both of your hearts. I am sure that we have all experienced this phenomenon in new relationships, but it can exist in long-term relationships as well. We are always able to re-establish these relationship roles through dating and we must maintain this through dating.

It is necessary to examine our history in order to create success in our future and not fall into the trap that most couples do. Once you have passed the honeymoon phase of your relationship it can often start to deteriorate whether you are aware of it or not. The honeymoon phase is quite simply the act of dating and courting with the passion of the relationship at its peak.

Realize that there are no reasons why the passion should disappear if you continue to put in the same effort that you did in the beginning of your relationship. I would advise you to look at what you truly did in the beginning of the courtship that allowed you to fall in love. More often than not, the same actions you took in the beginning of your romance will revitalize your level of passion to its original state.

Case Study: Ashley and Dave

Ashley was fresh out of a five-year relationship. It was easy to tell that she had an emotional connection to Dave, her ex. However, she had clearly made the decision that he was not going to be the one true love of her life. We were talking about what could have been done to rekindle their flame before she reached that terminal point.

Ante Up

She explained that they never had a formal "dating and courtship" period. They were long-time friends who entered into a romantic relationship. I asked more questions, there must have been something that led them into a romantic relationship. As we talked, it became clear that Ashley was attracted to Dave because of their friendship and how intensely he listened to her every word.

She had moved away and they put the relationship on hold, not sure what the future would hold. When she returned, Dave was a great friend who listened intently to all of her stories of adventures abroad. Within a few weeks, they were madly in love (again) and things were great.

But again, the romance faded, Dave stopped being fully present and became detached. She had enough, and threatened to break it off. Even though his attitude had change, he was still in love with Ashley and he went out of his way to make many grand gestures. The sorts of things that a man may do if he were courting a woman for the first time: flowers and notes and dates and surprises.

It felt contrived; everything he tried didn't fit into where their relationship had come from. It didn't feel that they were coming naturally from his heart but out of desperation. It still didn't rekindle the flame. What mattered to Ashley was the strength of their friendship. She didn't want flowers; she wanted her best friend back. If they had figured this out sooner, this story could have had a very different ending.

Among other roles in your relationship, your mate had better be one of your best friends if you intend to have lasting success.

Every relationship is different and unique, but there are always essential keys for success.

Life is always going to change. We need to be mindful of where we started and what dynamics truly allowed us to fall in love so we can always ensure they exist for true success.

Case Study 2: John and Diane

When John and Diane meet they both had very busy lives. They both ran their own successful companies and had little time for anything else let alone a relationship. Somehow they made time and their relationship grew, they got married. A few years later their jobs changed and they had some financial windfalls. All of a sudden they had so much time together that they really don't know what to do with one another. This led to an incredible imbalance and caused stress in ways that used to generate passion.

After interviewing the couple, I discovered where they had started from and now where they were. A new plan was created. John started volunteering two nights a week giving his time away in the profession that had afforded him the lifestyle he now enjoyed. He found quickly that the passion for his former career still burned brightly. Diane, on the same days, would ensure that she was busy late into the afternoons. She had always wanted to learn to golf and found a ladies group that met twice a week. The results were that for those two days every week, they wouldn't see each other from noon until late in the evening. They spent time doing the things they enjoyed and recharging themselves. Here's where the fun started, they began to play again and John started to do some of things he had done many years ago. He left love notes for her on his volunteer nights. They said things like:

> *Hi Honey,*
>
> *Hope you had a great day. I am really looking forward to seeing you at the end of my day and was wondering if you would like to go for a walk later. I noticed today on the calendar that it is a full moon and I thought it would be romantic. Be home by 10:20pm.*
>
> *Love, John.*

Sure, it's not Shakespeare but it reminds her of the things he used to do. When he got home she was waiting for him and they held hands as they walked and talked about their day. Reconnecting also reignites a passionate romance. At last count, John and Diane were acting like a couple of newlyweds enjoying playing with one another in many fashions.

There's a certain passion that comes with having a crazy schedule and knowing how precious every minute together is versus having the whole day, every day together. When time is plentiful, the need to plan isn't as great as when time is limited, or at least that is the perception.

You don't need to go backwards in your life and go back to a crazy lifestyle or job to inject some craziness into your romance, but maybe plan to be a little less predictable and not available all the time and see what happens. Encourage your partner to spend time with her friends or on a hobby she enjoys and you do the same. See if it works.

This helps recharge the polarity between you. Your intent is important here. Be careful not to make it look like you aren't interested in her or that you need to go off "by yourself." But by finding ways to re-create the conditions you felt when you first fell in love, you will start to understand what your version of dating and courtship really was. Taking the time to recharge your polarity will create new growth in your love and passion.

It's about creating your destiny. If you know exactly what you want, have a plan and execute it, you will attract exactly what you desire; the woman of your dreams. The woman you dream of is often the woman you have already chosen. You need to be the man that you were when she fell in love with you. Dating and courting are the simple solutions to growing and maintaining that *in-love* feeling forever; truly loving her and being loved with *massive untamed raw passion,* I know it's what I want from my relationship, don't you?

Once you start moving forward again, you can take some of the upcoming ideas and run wild with them, making magic everyday with the love of your life. Be patient.

CHALLENGE THREE

List three ways that you created time when you were courting the love of your life. We all had busy lives when we met but somehow we managed to fit it all in.

1. _____

2. _____

3. _____

Now what plans can you make to closely re-create similar situations in your life now?

1. _____

2. _____

3. _____

Chapter Four:

Cut to the chase: What do women really want?

"The objective of dating is to keep your lover in a state of bliss, where she feels beautiful in your eyes and appreciated in your heart."

Men are typically more analytical in decisions, versus women who lead with their hearts. This is very similar to our description of polarity of masculine and feminine energies. Most men are confused about exactly what a woman is looking for in an ideal man.

As men, we want to find ways to study and quantify what women want. Around the world, sociologists and psychologists have studied women. According to their findings, what women want is driven primarily by ancient DNA passed from one generation of women to the next, no matter what culture or country the women live in today. Most of the patterns involve the basic survival of the family unit and the desire for security and direction.

When I was interviewing women for this book, they expressed great excitement and interest in men acting on theses principles. Men, this means they want YOU, the ones reading this book. In my interviews, we discussed what women find attractive in men and what they want from men in relationship and in bed.

Yes, women do appreciate nice eyes, a great smile and a tight ass. It may not be true for all women, but when I asked about those three specific physical traits in my questionnaire, they giggled and smiled. Which I read to mean having great physical qualities doesn't hurt.

Your outer appearance aside, the most important qualities that I *continually* heard from women was that they all wanted a man who is **present** and **on purpose**. These are the new buzzwords. They don't want metrosexuals, they want men who are present and on purpose; men who will lead them somewhere in their love and in their life.

I was just starting to grasp what 'metro' really meant and then found out that women have gone and changed their minds. Women desiring metrosexuals was a short phase. Metrosexual's nice clothes and apt fitness are important traits in physical attraction, but it is easy to see that there needs to be more for a great relationship to from. It turns out that 'present and on purpose' is what women have loved since the beginning of time, just as the 'ologists' earlier stated.

What does present and on purpose mean:

Being present -- the ability to be authentic and be comfortable in your skin. Living in *this* moment and not distracted by what comes next. Fully engaged.

Being on Purpose -- knowing where you are going in life and acting on a plan that you execute daily to 100% of your ability. Understanding why you were put on this Earth.

These are good explanations but still in womanspeak. A man who is present is:

- ➢ Confident
- ➢ Certain
- ➢ Authentic
- ➢ Natural
- ➢ Attentive
- ➢ Observant
- ➢ Engaged

"It's when a man is just happy as he is. He's not trying to be anything or anyone he's not; he is living by his chosen terms. He is at ease with his surroundings and makes decisions taking into account all of his senses."

"He listens to everything said to him. He notices his surroundings. He is proud of the way he lives his life. He meets everyone with an open mind and knows how to speak from his heart. He is happy to be both in his own company as well as in the company of many. "

A man on purpose is:

- ➢ Self-motivated
- ➢ Decisive
- ➢ A problem solver

- Able to takes action
- Dependable
- A goal setter
- Able to evaluate his success
- Willing to learn

"A man on purpose is always heading in a specific direction. He is always aware of where he is and where he is going. He has a plan to get there and is willing to change if he is not getting the result he wants. A man that can make decisions is attractive to women."

One of the easiest areas for us to showcase our ability to be present and on purpose is the way we pursue our woman when it comes to dating. Women want to feel that they are "on your train" and you will lead them somewhere. Here are two ways to ask a woman out – which is more on purpose, which is more effective?

"Would you like to do something some time?"

or

"Would you like to join me on a fantastic night to give us a chance to get to know each other a little better? I can't give you all of the details, but tonight, I'll email you. We could get together on Thursday night. We'll have an incredible time together. Can I look forward to your company?"

Maybe the last question is a little over the top, but what do you think the response would be? The first question is weak and has no real direction. It's like fishing without a hook. The second is detailed and direct. It states a goal; to get to know each other. It is time limited; Thursday night. It is mysterious without all the information; like fishing with a baited hook. It's heartfelt and shows some serious intention around pursuing this woman. If she is at all interested, she will be there on Thursday, or beg for a different night. If not, then at least you know she's not really interested in you.

I know many couples who fall victim to the first question. I also know people that have a "date night" once a week. This is a great idea in theory, but can be equally destructive as constructive, depending on how you plan and execute these outings.

Most couples will wait until that said day arrives before they decide how to spend this time. They go to their favorite spot for dinner or rent a movie or something of that nature. How different would the week go if, at the beginning of the week, the man sends a package to his love with a note saying:

I can't wait to spend time with you on our date night. I have everything planned and I ask that you to be dressed to the nines and ready at 6 o'clock for an incredible evening. Here are some chocolate kisses to enjoy. Every one of the chocolates represents one of the kisses you will receive during the evening. I will warn you that they may not all be on your lips... Please don't ask anything else about our date night; I won't give you any more information. I love you. See you tonight.

What do you think the relationship will look like in the week leading up to that date night? There will be a lot more flirtatious moments: longer and deeper kissing sessions before bed, flirty touching when you pass by each other at home and maybe a nice phone call during the day while you are at work.

All of the magical little things called **courtship** will reappear in your romance. There will be excitement in the air with the anticipation of this pre-planned date. This is something you should keep as a random ritual. Every week is overkill, but once or twice every month is just about right. The objective of dating your lover is to keep her blissful so she feels beautiful in your eyes and appreciated in your heart. The planning and taking action will prove to her that you are on purpose with your romance with her.

Just starting this plan is enough; by the end of this book you will know how to make a perfect date. Everything you are or want to be great at needs both planning and time. Why would a successful relationship be any different?

So, in a relationship, women want men to be on purpose and present. It really hasn't changed that much. It used to be about a man's ability to provide food and shelter for his family. Now she can provide for herself financially if she wants. Now you need to provide for your family emotionally. Be there to lead the direction of the romance and the direction of the family. Make a difference.

Live your divine purpose and give from the deepest parts of your heart and soul. Times have changed. We no longer need to hunt for food. So how do you become this incredible man who is desired by your woman?

CHALLENGE FOUR

What can you do to be more present right now? What can you do to be more focused on the people you interact with? How do you like people to be present with you? List five things you can do to be more present with everyone: your woman, you friends, you co-workers.

1. _____

2. _____

3. _____

4. _____

5. _____

What is your purpose? If you can find something that you love to do and can convince someone to pay you to do it, chances are, it's what you should be doing for a living. List three things you love to do and if they are not present in your life, create a simple plan to bring them into your life. Playing in your passions will reveal your true purpose.

Passion   Plan

1. _____   _____
                   _____

2. _____   _____
                   _____

3. _____   _____
                   _____

Chapter Five:

Thank You Sir John McCallum – Gentlemen's Training

I lost my father when I was four years old. It never ceases to amaze me how the universe provides exactly what you need, exactly when you need it. By the time I was eight, I was fortunate enough to have a new neighbor at the end of my street. John McCallum, a divorcé with his three almost-grown children, moved in. He would become both my friend and my teacher and he was a true "old world" gentlemen.

When I first met John, he was silver-haired and already into his early 50s. He was born and raised in Scotland and by the time he was in his early 20s had already served in the Royal Regiment. His upbringing and his time in the service made John an amazing man and gave him an incredible appreciation for women. He had the ability to care for women in a way that inspired them to fully be in their feminine energy. There were many specific lessons he taught me, but more important was the modeling I witnessed as John courted my mother and found a place in our family. His lessons are both timeless and priceless. John's example laid down the foundation for me to become the kind of man that women appreciate and desire. I am grateful for all of his teachings and grace.

Patience

With my developmental years being absent of a male presence, there were definitely a few sports that John felt I needed to be educated on immediately. The first was fishing and the second was golf. If there were ever two sports that teach patience, these were them. Fishing is all guesstimating exactly the best time and place to catch the fish. Ultimately though, it's up to the fish to grab your hook. Isn't it funny how that sounds like "trolling" for women.

Golf is about chasing a little white ball all over hell's half acre and waiting for those golden moments when you finally hit the perfect shot. Interestingly enough, this too mirrors courtship. Doing whatever it takes for the possibility of gaining that first perfect kiss.

My greater lesson in patience came from observing John pining after my mother for years. Although my mother's intent was made clear from the onset, it was this gentleman's diligence that was proof to her that he was a man worthy of her attention and affections.

All I know is that after a few years they started traveling together. Quite frankly, I don't need to know the details, but it was easy to tell that his patience prevailed. He first sought out amazing friendships with my mother, my sister and me. Second, he found ways to give from his heart. These were things like helping with odd tasks around our house that maybe my mother didn't like to do, taking interest into her children's lives and including all of us in his passions for cooking and sports. He simply lived his life the best way he knew how and then let time soften my mother's heart.

Being on Purpose

We've agreed that a man without purpose is like a ship lost at sea, it may never find its way. It has no real use to anyone. A man who is living his purpose; a man who has specific goals and an action plan to achieve all of those goals are the traits that women find most attractive in men. John was a man who was proud of his career. He sold screws for construction projects all over the world. It challenged him daily and afforded him the lifestyle he enjoyed. He felt as though he was making a difference. He continually set short-term and long-term goals that he knew would help him to achieve the next level in his company within a set time frame.

He would share these goals with my family as a way of holding himself accountable. When he achieved his goals he would happily share the news and always invited us to celebrate those wins with him. I'm sure that he took some joy in having us rejoice in his victories, but he was also continually proving to us that he was a man of his word. Over time, we all came to expect that if John said he was going to do something, then it was actually going to be completed. We also came to trust the decisions that John would make regarding his path in life. It was easy to trust that he would also always make good decisions regarding our family's well being.

We don't always know exactly what our purpose is in life... but if you don't yet know, commit to finding your purpose. You can take time everyday to sit in silence until you start to feel the right answer. It's amazing how silence and an open mind will help bring clarity and allow you to hear your inner self talking to you about what you should be focusing on in life.

It won't necessarily always be your career. It could be to focus on being an incredible husband or father, or to chase a dream of yours that may lead you to true happiness, or your purpose could simply be whatever makes you feel the most complete when you are doing it. It is different for every man and everyone must discover it for himself. No one can answer this one for you, only you can. You may even find your purpose and pursue it for a while, then wake up one morning and feel it isn't right for you anymore. That's OK. Just start the process of discovery again.

Go First Class

John had a simple expression that he has always lived by, "It only costs a little extra to go first class." It's the difference between ordering four glasses of house wine or paying an extra three dollars to have a bottle on your table; both are the same volume of wine. It's the difference between buying the cheap seats for a concert and investing the little extra so that you are close enough to actually see the expressions on the artist's face. The contrast between ordering a limousine to take you to the airport on your way to your vacation versus taking a taxicab is momentous in setting the tone for the trip.

I'm not suggesting that you spend copious amounts of money to impress anybody, ever. Although, it is often the case that just a few more dollars may create a lasting memory that could otherwise be missed. It makes the people in your life feel as though they are greatly cared for and portrays the fact that you expect only the best for them and yourself in your life.

Dress with Purpose

John always understood the importance of dressing to impress. To work, he would always wear a crisply ironed shirt and a stylish suit that would include a monogrammed handkerchief. He would come home at the end of the day and change into a pair jeans and a polo shirt. If we were all heading out for dinner that evening, again, he would change into something a little classier, perhaps swapping the polo for a casual button-down shirt with the sleeves turned up. Regardless of what he was doing he always wanted to look his best and be appropriate for the moment.

It's a cliché that clothes make the man but I'm sure that you've experienced putting on a new suit or pair of jeans and instantly having a physiological change that magically allows you to stand a little taller and breathe a little deeper. Just spend the afternoon sometime shopping for a new suit. You don't necessarily need to buy anything, just go and play a little. Try on a bunch of amazing clothes and see how you feel. It is absolute truth that taking pride in what you are wearing will have positive effects in multiple areas of your life.

If you have no clue as to what is currently in style, grab some men's magazines. Or spend a little time on the internet and you'll find countless examples of both current and timeless styles. If you're still having a hard time, find someone who you know to be stylish and simply ask for their advice. If you are in a relationship, you could ask her for her opinion, after all, she's the one you are trying to impress. Invite her out for an afternoon of shopping and offer a lovely lunch to thank her for her help. Most people will be completely flattered you considered them with something as important as your style and image.

If you're concerned about the financial strain of buying a few new power pieces of clothing, it may be useful to know that there are several outlet stores for all major brands of clothing and department stores. Stores like Nordstrom's Rack have quality brand names at great low prices. You can go to thrift stores in affluent neighbourhoods and will find the quality of merchandise to be outstanding and of incredible value.

Another great idea if you are serious about addressing your look is to engage your shopping partner and invite them over to your house to go through your closet with you. Let me give you a little advice that will save you some embarrassment for when they arrive. With the exception of some casual fashion jeans, anything with a hole in it (especially socks and gonch) are all garbage. Any shirts that are pit stained are garbage. All clothing that is either excessively too large or too small for you, give to the thrift store so somebody else can enjoy them.

Don't take what you hear personally. It is in your best interest and you have asked this person for their advice based on their informed opinion. Honour that opinion.

When it comes to dating, a woman will always notice what you are wearing. If she can tell that you have made that little extra effort, it will definitely increase your attractiveness in her eyes and let her know that you take pride in yourself. It all goes back to the idea that clothes do in fact make the man.

Scents make sense

The Scent of a Woman is a truly great movie, but the scent of a man can anchor incredible memories within a woman. John only ever had two colognes. One scent that he would wear every day to work, and the second scent that he would put on whenever he went anywhere with my mother. It is amazing how sensitive a woman's response is to smell.

If you wear the same cologne on amazing dates that you create with a woman, anytime you wear that cologne she will immediately have a positive change in physiology. She will immediately start to smile and have an increase in her body temperature; all good signs for you. So go to a shop and try some different scents and ask for some advice from any and all the women around the area. Just simply ask them for an opinion and tell them that you are trying to attract the woman of your dreams. I have never met a woman that wasn't willing to help you in attracting your true love. It will be good for your confidence and ego to have some interaction with women.

Beyond colognes, there are a plethora of other smells that you can introduce into your relationship. If you take a trip down to your local aromatherapy shop, you will be amazed at the science of smell that they will be able to educate you on. There are candles and oils that can encourage everything from relaxation to heightened sexual awareness. Next time you are shopping with your love, go and smell some scents and find out what she likes. Then go and buy some massage oil with that scent. When you're washing your bed sheets, you can add scented dryer sheets to create a slumber haven. If you have shoes at home that may not smell as fresh as they should, you can also take those dryer sheets and fire those into the shoes; challenge overcome. If you ask at that aromatherapy shop, a few drops of certain oils like peppermint or eucalyptus will kill nasty odours as well. The little attention to details will all add up.

Time is a Gift

Lessons from the golf course; if you miss your tee time there will not often be another for quite some time. Apply this to everywhere in your life. If you say you will be somewhere at a certain time and you miss that time commitment, you must be prepared to face the consequence. Another opportunity may not come around again for quite some time. Be impeccable with your time commitments, and the woman as well as all of the people in your life will come to know you as a trustworthy person. Furthermore, you will begin to trust yourself.

I will give you a simple challenge for the next 30 days. When you set your alarm clock to wake up the following morning, get up as soon as it goes off. Don't hit the snooze bar and don't reset the time. Watch how creating a simple routine in your life can transform so many other areas. In a very short period of time you will learn that the extra 30 minutes of sleep you thought you needed has not been missed. Furthermore, you will have time to do all the things you want to in the morning. If you get ready with time to spare, use this time to catch up on the news or write an email to a family member, extra time is a great gift if spent well.

Never Let Them See You Sweat

As a great example of a man for me to model growing up, John always had a plan for any activity. What I didn't realize until years later, was that there was always some flexibility, as well as a backup plan. I remember going on vacation together. My dear mother was famous for being casually late to almost everything, including airplanes. John had incredible foresight into the situation. We live about a 45-minute drive from the airport and our international flight was leaving in two hours. Without a hint of frustration or anger in his voice he assisted our entire family as best he could to get us out of the house as quickly as possible. Now with only 90 minutes until our flight was due to leave, we were just pulling out of our driveway. As you know with all international flights, you must check in two hours prior to departure time and clearly we were not going to make it. John took the initiative to call the airline and let them know that we had just had a small emergency and would be arriving with great haste. He had the airline arrange valet parking for us when we arrived at the airport, as well as a porter to aid us with our bags. He checked us in over the phone and all he needed to do was show our passports on arrival. Our bags were hand loaded on the flight after everyone boarded the plane and we had to run to the gate as they were holding the doors open for us. Later, I found out that John had already had another flight arranged for us if we missed the first one. Always having a backup plan, if needed, is a stroke of genius.

We are not always in control of other people and not everything goes to plan. The airplane story is a shining example of how a great man deals with challenge. Stay focused on what outcome you want, keep your ego and cool in check and go about finding the best solutions. There is always a way to have everything you want in your life, even with obstacles that arise.

Choose Your Reaction

This is the second part of the story of the airplane. John's reaction to us being excessively late for the beginning of vacation would have most likely infuriated most men. Instead of acting on that frustration he chose to love my mother's idiosyncrasy. Embracing her craziness, he made accommodations so that we could all have an amazing beginning to our vacation and probably created the strongest memory of that vacation.

How many of you, have at one time or another had to wait an extraordinary amount of time for a woman to get ready? We all have the ability to decide how we wish to react to the situation. Most negative reactions will create massive stress between you and your date, which will inevitably lead to a rocky start to your adventure. If you take the time to have some flexibility in your plans for the evening, then it is easy to rejoice in the fact that there is a woman taking time to make herself as beautiful as possible for you. With this outlook, you will remain relaxed and simply give the space and time that she requires to do whatever it is that they do when getting ready. Pour a glass of wine, read a magazine, surf the net — keep yourself busy so she does feel as though you are sitting there getting upset. Reassure her that you are content and there is no real rush. Adjust your plans accordingly.

Choosing your reaction and building flexibility is key in relationships as well as in all other areas of your life. Things always happen that we can't control, but we can react in any manner we wish. We have the choice to live in love or live in fear. These two options will ultimately lead us to all decisions including our reactions to life. Living in a place of fear is when we are solely focused on ourselves. When you are so worried about what will happen to you in every instance then this will result in you going into survival mode. All decisions made in fear are based on self preservation. When you react from a place of love, you look for ways to live that will be beneficial for everyone. You step back from challenges and see the entire picture before you react. You realize the true value of all situations and act accordingly. The choice is yours and it is all up to you.

Chivalry is Alive and Well

Every door should be held open every time for every person. John would never miss one unless I beat him to it. It was almost a game that we would play as a way of ingraining this habit into my life. Ladies should always come first before you: when you're pouring a bottle of wine, serving food, exiting an elevator, or allowing her to queue up in the bank line when you both arrive at roughly the same time. When you're out for dinner you assist your date into her seat before you sit and every time she goes to leave the table do the little half stand up. Assist her into her seat again when she returns. This little sequence of moves through dinner as well as all the acts of chivalry are never intended to be anything more than gracious, small, quiet moments of respect and appreciation for the woman in your life. Do not attempt to draw too much attention to yourself while doing these or they may backfire.

In fact, I've had some women take a slight offense to acts of chivalry. I've spent time with some women who make it difficult for me to engage in these acts as they are continually opening their own doors and being completely self-sufficient. Trust me; I completely understand that women do not need anything from a man. But if we are on a date, there must be a preference from that woman to have a man in her life.

As I mentioned before, there are some characteristics that women are looking for in men and one of these of course, is a strong quiet confidence. When you come across a very strong willed woman, you have the golden opportunity to win her over through your actions and words. At some point after going through a door she opened for you, find somewhere you could stop for a moment, turn and face her completely straight on and then look directly into her eyes and say, "I would appreciate your help with something. I try to be a complete gentleman all of the time. One of the things that I greatly enjoy doing is opening doors for you. It's not that I believe you can't do it yourself but it is my way of showing just a small appreciation for all of the beautiful softness and feminine energy that lives within you. Would you allow me this honour?"

I would expect after asking so graciously that for the rest of the evening every time you open a door you'll find a soft smile playing around the lips of your companion. Congratulations, you've just scored 10,000 points in the dating game. Now if after saying something similar to this statement your date does not have a smile on her face but instead wants to debate, I suggest you just turn and run away. If a woman cannot even allow you to open a door for her, then she's clearly not ready for any type of relationship as she has not yet made room to have a man in her life. If you do end up in a debate, you can happily quote me on it.

These chivalrous acts are small examples of how a man should take care of woman in life. Whether or not a woman ever really does need any taking care of is of little importance, but the notion that we would and could take care of a woman from a place of joy and love is truly epic in her eyes. So have fun with this, play within the old code. As an example, every time I wish a woman to go before me in a line or through of a door, I simply stop and make a small two-handed gesture to open the way for her. I may also add a little French wording, along with the gesture and simply say Mademoiselle. Be creative and know that these little acts allow you to shine as a gentleman.

ABC – Always Be Clean

Once a week without fail, John would drive his Buick Regal down to the car wash. It became a bit of a ritual that on Sunday mornings we would go and clean the car, both inside and out. It's amazing how much you can tell about a man by the state of his car. If it is kept clean and tidy and the gas tank is full enough to go anywhere, chances are, this is a man who is organized in his life and knows exactly where is he is going and is prepared for just about anything.

Keep your home clean. This means cleaning the bathroom top to bottom once a week, vacuuming the floors or sweeping up bi-weekly, never having more than three dishes in the sink, making your bed daily, putting away your laundry and dusting the entire place at least once a month. The benefits to this are immeasurable. You will enjoy spending time in your home. You never know when your date might be coming home with you. If you live with your date, these practices are a necessity to show the simple respect of sharing space with someone. We know how much women appreciate men when they just take charge, and this is one area of our lives that is a mandatory. Women notice everything: please don't allow them to notice the stinky socks curled up under your bed. These acts of cleanliness speak directly to your character, and there is no excuse to not get top marks in this area of your life.

For Your Eyes Only

John always really spoke to me. He showed me the greatest respect by simply looking directly into my eyes when we were having a conversation. It never mattered to him what age I was, he treated me like a great friend. My greatest friends always look me in the eyes when we have real conversations.

There is something else that happens when you look someone straight in their eyes. You can no longer hide from them and they have a direct connection to your heart and visa versa. If you have spent any time around kids, you know what it means to have someone speak to your heart. Up to a certain age, kids speak only from their hearts. There is something that happens as we grow up that makes us want to become very private. It happens about the same age that you no longer want your mom to see you naked, when you are around six years old. It was about the same time I became "funny." For me, humour was a deflector to guard my heart and keep me safe from anyone really getting to know me that well. People still liked me, and I was a good friend with a sense of humor, but I put my guard up.

Learning to open my heart, through eye contact and being open to other people's heart was a valuable lesson. You need to start looking into people's eyes every time you are communicating with them (words are optional). I could intuitively feel and or read people at a much deeper level. Sometimes I feel as though there are things I just needed to say to them and I don't always know where the words would come from.

One time, I had met a woman in a group that I was working with and I went up to her. I asked her if I could tell her something that didn't make any sense to me but it may to her. The words, "Your son is fine," came flying out of my mouth before I even knew if she wanted to hear them. She started to cry. It freaked me out. It turned out that her son had been away traveling in a foreign country for a few weeks and she had yet to hear from him. I cannot tell you how this works, or why, but I dare you to start looking into people's eyes and trying to connect to their hearts and see what happens.

In relationships, learning and practicing to speak with your eyes locked with your partner's will transform the way you speak to her heart. When your woman can start to really believe all of the things that you say are from your heart, she will trust you to the nth degree. If you want to fully regain the heart you are chasing, you need that trust. Your intimacy will reach a new level if you practice this.

Growing, Growing, Gone

If something is not growing, it's dying. This is an absolute truth. If your intention is to be an incredible man you always need to be learning something new. My gentleman teacher always had a book on his bedside table. He actually read them. He explored business or how to better interact with people or cultural differences. He always wanted to be at his best.

Choose one or two areas of your life that you wish to evolve in. From there, find ways to access new knowledge. Take audio books from your local library or download via your computer for a small cost. I load these onto my iPod and, when I'm working out or driving, I take this time and use it constructively. This can be a great way to learn new languages, take on new information in an area of personal development, or even enjoy a great piece of fiction.

If you really want to evolve quickly in an area of your life, I strongly suggest you get a coach or a mentor. These people will be able to quickly and accurately give you all of the information you require to grow to your desired potential, as well as be able to give you truthful feedback to increase the rate at which you transform. You need to weigh whether the cost of a professional is worth the time you require to actually get what you want. Using a professional will not only save time, but often money in the long run.

Another incredible way to grow towards your best is to volunteer some of your time. Find organizations that would be happy to have your help for a specific amount of time, so that you can make and honor that commitment to its fullest. I would suggest you find an area that you truly enjoy working in so you can shine as a great example of a man to all those involved. It is amazing that you will often find that the giving of yourself is far more rewarding than any effort that you put forth. This is a true win-win situation.

If you've never volunteered before, here are a few things you can do: skiing instruction for disabled skiers, first aid attendant at musical festivals, coaching youth sports including golf, baseball and ice hockey, or being a welcome greeter at a wine show. Find something you love and make a few phone calls, free help is almost never turned away. Volunteers often state that they get a lot more than they ever give. Learning new skills, being put in a different culture and meeting and networking with people that you may not have otherwise ever had contact with, these are all ways to stretch and grow.

Extra Extra

Every morning before work, John would sit down with his morning coffee and flip through the daily newspaper. As a man, it is of great importance to be worldly and be aware of what's going on around you. Not only are there tremendous benefits in your business life to being aware of world trends, but it allow you to engage in intelligent conversations. When you are on a date with the woman of your dreams, it is brilliant to be able to share views and sometimes even debate current events a little bit. If she is not up on these events, take time to explain the ones that you are passionate about without being condescending. It will give her an opportunity to learn more about your insights and she will feel secure that you are the kind of man that has a pulse on all the things important to his life.

If you are not likely to read the paper everyday or tune into your local news stations, make the homepage of your internet browser, one of the big news sources: CNN is good and BBC is better.

Healing Through Health

John was never as fit as he would have wanted to be, but he was always working towards it. This is one of your areas of life that having a plan of action is just as important as achieving your goals.

There are so many quick-fix diets and gimmicks and infomercials late at night, which all promise you instant results. The road to wellness is surprisingly easy. This is just about everything you need to know to have a healthy life. It is more about common sense than anything else.

1. Breathe. I mean really breathe. The program is simple. At least three times a day, take 10 deep and powerful breaths as follows: inhale for a count, hold four counts and exhale for two counts. To start with, try a four-second inhale fully using your diaphragm, hold for 16 seconds and exhale for eight seconds pushing out all the air in your lungs using your abdomen. If this is too easy, adjust times to make it more challenging but not hard. Increase numbers as you become stronger. You will think clearer, lower your stress level, strengthen your cardio ability and even lose weight through simply breathing.

2. Eat an equal or greater amount of raw organic food as you do "dead" food (Do a search of raw food if you need more information). Be mindful of your total calorie intake every day. The average man needs between 2,000 and 2,500 calories per day based on body size and exercise. If you are in excess of these numbers, every 3,500 calories over will put an extra pound on your body. I am not saying you should obsess about counting, but become aware of where crazy calories come from. A fast food lunch combo meal is often between 1,000 and 1,500 calories which is half your daily intake. Add a large caramel blended frozen coffee (500 calories) and two chocolate-chunk cookies for an afternoon snack (480 calories) and your intake should

be done for the day. Except for the fact that you haven't had dinner (more than 800 calories), a glass of wine (85 calories) or a beer (165 calories) and the whipped cream you intend to lick off your naked partner's body in your bed later (599 calories per can). Learn a little, observe regularly and misbehave occasionally. All nutritional information is easily searched these days; check out the calories in salad dressing and soda, you will be surprised by the results.

3. Exercise at least three times a week. My definition of exercise is simple, if you're not sweating for more than 20 minutes, it doesn't count. Sweating is an incredible way to detoxify your body. If you have specific goals in mind, get with a health professional or sports trainer to build a program for you. You will save time and energy and be able to achieve those goals in a healthy safe way. If you are working out and getting injured or are always sore, you need some professional help.

4. Get started on a health supplement program. Chances are, you've done damage to your body, and you aren't aware that it needs to be fixed. I would recommend that you find a health food store or supplement distributor you trust. When I started taking supplements, not only did my overall energy and health increase, but I was also able to overcome the asthma that I'd been living with for over 33 years. Supplements can change your life for the better.

5. Find ways to eliminate as much stress in your life as possible. Studies continually show that stress is one of the biggest contributors to all forms of illness from the common cold to cancer. You either need to find ways to deal with the stress that you have or physically remove it from your life.

6. Laugh every single day. Find something that causes you to have one of those amazing belly laughs once a day. It is believed laughing will give you incredible health. I know people that have cured cancer through laughing it out of their bodies. The key to making this work is to simply allow yourself to laugh out loud at those email jokes that get passed around, or read the comics in the newspaper and if it is funny, really laugh. I believe that most people are embarrassed by laughter in public. Just GO for it. Laughter is contagious and you can make the people around you healthier at the same time.

Obviously there are more things you can do to increase the quality of your health and your life. These are the first six simple, easy-to-live-by guidelines. You may know all of these, but practicing them is completely different.

You may also want to consider getting some professional help. We all have a past that is affecting the way that we live our lives today. We have old beliefs that may not coincide with our current paths. Almost all of us have unresolved issues from our childhood or young adulthood that have not come to complete closure yet. Don't spend years dwelling on this—just get it sorted and watch your life change. Go to some personal development programs or get a shrink. Take some action to move away from the past and into the future.

Taking care of yourself both physically and mentally will transform your confidence in all the parts of your life. You will walk taller when your muscles are a little tight from working out. You will breathe deeper when your inner body is working better than ever before. You will be able to give from a deeper place when you are not weighed down by life. You will live longer and be much happier when you put it all together.

Keep Your Eyes on Your Target

I learned to keep my eyes on my target from John's focus on my mother. I didn't realize these lessons until I had already destroyed my first marriage. So... here are the goods. You need to understand this lesson.

When you are with a woman or in a relationship you need to only see that woman intimately. As you move through your days in the world, you need to train yourself to not be fed by the sexual energy of other women. Only allow your partner to be your source of sexual energy.

If you think back to the beginning of a relationship in your life, I am sure you can recall that when you first met her, an incredible thing happened. All of the other women in the world magically disappeared. You could have been walking down the street with your sweetheart on your arm and the Swedish national bikini squad could have walked in front of you. You would have entirely missed the fact that they were all blowing you kisses and handing out telephone numbers. That is what focusing on the woman in your life is like.

Over time our intense focus fades. We start to notice all of the sexual energy that is being infused out of our lives with every turn we take. Image your sexual energy as the fuel tank in your car. Once you have emptied your tank there is nothing more to give and the car has no drive. Each day, we start with a full tank of sexual energy. We can choose to spend it or have it all spent for us. That may be something few of you have considered. But every time you look at any woman and have a sexual thought in your head, you are spending that energy. Maybe you're looking forward to your drive to work because you always see this beautiful woman who runs down your street at the same time every day. Or maybe there's a woman at work that you look forward to seeing because she has amazing legs and always wears a skirt that is just a little shorter than it should be to be professional. Consider how sports events on TV are loaded with commercials that feature scantily dressed women. These are all areas where we may spend too much focus, which can dilute and destroy the passion with your partner sexually and intimately.

I have a challenge for you. Tomorrow, count how many woman you see sexually. I don't mean the ones that you interact with in your daily life. If your eye wanders towards anyone's "bathing suit" areas, then that woman counts as one. If you need to see the face of a woman you don't know, just to see if she is pretty or young, count that as another one. You may be amazed at the number you reach. Every one of those images are using up your sexual energy tank.

I used to check out every car that I passed when I was driving. At every stoplight I would always roll up to the next car to see if there was someone nice to look at. I found that I was so addicted to checking woman out that it was no wonder that my tank felt low at the end of the day. It got to a point that I started to wonder if my libido was getting lower because of my age.

So let's get rid of some clichés. Men do not hit their sexual peak at 18 or 19. Your sexuality may never peak but keeps getting stronger through gaining new sexual knowledge and engaging your partner to her fullest. Your sex life doesn't have to disappear after you get married or after having kids. It is a choice. It is about re-training yourself.

So how does it all work? This is where the work comes in. You have the ability to retrain your eyes. You can actually train yourself to not see all of the things that suck the sexual energy from you. After the exercise of counting the number of women you notice in a day, you should have a clue to where you lose your energy. Make a mental list of as many of the daily rituals that deplete your sexual energy and eliminate them from your life. Stop all of these activities immediately. Remind yourself from your experiment of all the places you saw sexual images: TV, movies, media, sidewalks, internet, and porn sites.

Media is usually the worst offender. If we watch TV or when we are on the internet, we are continually bombarded with sexual images. You must make a new practice of recognizing these images and then immediately bouncing your eyes away from them. If you are watching TV, physically move your head in a different direction until the image has passed. You may find that some shows are just too difficult to watch. When you are sure an image is gone, continue watching your show. Do the same thing for movies. If a billboard, while you are driving, is drawing your energy, deflect your eyes to the car in front of you. That is probably where your eyes should be anyway. If you are walking down the street and catch yourself fantasizing about the girl walking past you, look at the pavement as fast as you can. This is all good practice and in time you will do it naturally.

After a while, you will be able to look at women without having those wild random sexual impulses. And then you can go back to watching all of a movie, without the self editing. But it's natural to slip up now and again. I practice "control" the first week of every month and after that I'm good to go for the rest of that month.

If you are asking yourself, "So why do all of this crap!!!" then you are trying to get out of having to do the work. So what's in it for you? Try it for 90 days and see how it affects your relationships. First off, you will have a crazy amount of energy for your everyday life. Your sexual energy and your actual energy are directly proportional. You will have a higher sexual attraction to the woman in your life. You will feel like you did in the beginning of your relationship. You will look forward to seeing her so she may satisfy your need to empty that tank.

Your tank will be filled not just by sexual acts, but in the smiles she give you, the kisses you share, the way you touch her as she moves by you after dinner, the looks you shoot her across the room and, yes, the way you can't wait to have her in your arms at the end of the day. Your intimacy will change overnight. You will be reconnected. She will be again the most beautiful woman you know and the only woman you crave.

If you are brave and committed, after a few weeks, tell your partner what you are doing. Tell her you have been focusing all of your energy on her so that you can increase your connection as a couple. Let her know that you are saving all of your sexual energy for her and that you didn't realize how it was being misspent. Don't go into too much detail. Let your woman know your shift in positive direction and focus on the future. Let her know that she is the only woman that you can see with sexual eyes and that you are committed to maintaining this discipline to further strengthen your relationship.

If you do this, be warned. She will test you at every turn. So get good at averting your eyes. After enough testing she will realize that you are a man of your word. She will be honored that you have made this decision to fully be in your partnership. You will evolve to a place in your relationship that you have not seen since you first started dating.

Remember Gratitude

So thank you, Sir John McCallum. I have always considered you a knight that was sent into my life to give me the lessons of how to become a great man. The quest to become a great man is one that will never end. John would be honored to know that the lessons he taught me are now being passed on to all of you. There is a great difference between knowing something and living something. Seize this opportunity and take on the challenge to live to your fullest. This is the only way to access all that you are capable of as well as having the effect of drawing amazing people into your life and having the ability to hold onto them. This could also include engaging a new woman to your life or perhaps rekindling a relationship that you have been in for quite some time.

CHALLENGE FIVE

Part A – Tomorrow, take note of how many sexual images and thoughts you actually get bombarded with in a day. Anytime you have a sexual thought about anyone beyond your partner or catch yourself looking at bathing suit areas count one point.

What's your score? _____

Part B – Identify where you saw most of the images and had most of your thoughts. Were they while you were driving, on the internet or watching TV? By identifying the challenge areas for yourself, the heightened awareness can help you to avoid these areas and be highly aware of when you need to deflect you eyes.

1. _____

2. _____

3. _____

Part C -- Commit for the next 90 days.

I, _____, fully commit to 100% of my ability, to deflect my eyes whenever I start spending my sexual energy on anything or anyone other than my partner. I will continue learning this practice from today, _____, for a minimum period of 90 days.

Chapter Six:

How to Win Your Woman's Heart

"The best proof of love is trust."

-Dr. Joyce Brothers

How do you win a woman's heart? It's about proving you are a purposeful man that can be trusted. Most men and women aren't conscious of this fact.

Women measure a man's trustworthiness by watching the way he lives his life and every action he makes. We gain that trust by simply saying what we mean and meaning what we say, as well as following through on every commitment. Whether it is showing up on time for a date or getting out of bed when the alarm clock goes off, the little things all add up. These prove to a woman how you would take care of her and a future family. When a woman trusts that you can take care of her, she will move into her pure feminine energy. Then you will really understand what polarity is all about. She will trust you to make decisions in your lives together. From grocery shopping to vacations, to planning the perfect anniversary party after you have been together for 25 years, she will believe in your abilities to provide for the both of you and that you will always guard her heart with your life.

If a relationship is like a train, then a woman just simply wants to get on board one that is actually going somewhere. The train (the man) has to be going in a forward motion and be set on a track destined for a specific place to arrive at a certain time. Trains that are stuck in the station are not generally acceptable. Over time a train may change tracks and or destinations, but the train cannot stop moving for anytime longer then his scheduled station stops. This all goes back to a man being on purpose in his life. If a woman is aware of a man's path and sees that he is regularly achieving his goals, there are even more reasons to trust him. Once you have captured a woman's heart, one of the keys to keeping it is to continue on your path of complete trustworthiness. Be that one person that she can count on for anything and everything at any time.

While you are continually dating the woman of your dreams, there is an amazing opportunity to allow the trust to grow. Let's look at a dinner date as an example of many opportunities. First of all, be ready on time. Next, have a reservation to wherever you are going. I know this may sound like a small detail but it shows that you planned something and then followed through with that decision.

Make a decision on which wine. Wine is one of those things you just need to know about as a man. You need to know a little bit about types of grapes and how those differences typically affect the food you are eating. You don't necessarily need to know about vintage and all the wine *frou frou* words, but you need to know at least which whites and reds are good companions for certain foods.

A pinot gris won't stand up to a steak, and a zinfandel would be perfect for a red sauce pasta dish. I make this point about needing to know your wines because it is such an easy way to build trust and take care of a woman. If you don't know anything about wine or need a little brush up, get on the internet or go to a wine tasting somewhere and figure it out. When you are out for dinner, if you can take a wine list and make a decision for the two of you, it's like getting extra points for nothing. Don't be afraid to ask a few questions of your date regarding what she is thinking of for dinner, or if she prefers a red or white, but that's it. Make the decision and let her be in awe of your abilities to be amazing. Beside a dinner date, wine is sexy and a really easy date anytime. Grab a bottle of something and a couple of takeout cups and you can go to just about any public place and enjoy each other's company and a little vino. If you choose not to drink alcohol, know a little about non-alcoholic wines and champagnes. Most restaurants will support you bringing in a bottle if they don't offer it in their restaurant, it doesn't infringe upon most liquor laws. It's still romantic and shows great planning.

Back to the date at hand, don't miss the opportunity to be a complete gentleman: every door opened every time; helping her into her chair at the table; standing every time she gets up from the table and when she returns. If you are not sure what I mean, re-watch the movie Pretty Woman. There is a scene where Julia Roberts is out for dinner with a group of men, and they all do this little move. I know we have talked about all of these before, but it is that important. So do it. Be the chivalrous man.

When it comes time for dessert, suggest sharing one. Ask for her input and then order it. Ask for two forks. Take care of small details, it's just another example of trusting your ability to take care of your woman.

At the end of the dinner, help your date into her jacket. Your next opportunity which is often missed is when you arrive back home. Open the door of the car for your date, just like you did every other door all night.

Take every opportunity on the date to prove you are trustworthy. Having a woman's heart will be your reward. The process of always living from a place of trust will affect other areas of your life. Your friendship with other men will deepen when they know you to be a man of your word. Your family will treat you differently when they know, without doubt, that you are a stand-up guy and will always be there for them. But the biggest pay-off is that you will believe in yourself and your ability to manifest your destiny, take action to your plans and live by your terms.

CHALLENGE SIX

This challenge is all about trusting yourself. Here are three specific tasks to accomplish everyday for the next 21 days. Prove to yourself that you can do anything you put your mind to. If you miss a day, just start the 21-day cycle the next day. You can do it.

1. Floss you teeth twice a day

2. Set your alarm clock to whatever time you need to be up the next day. Don't hit the SNOOZE BAR! Hear the alarm and get up. Even on your days off.

3. Every day at a specific time, I want you to call someone you know and tell them why they are important in your life. It can be short and sweet; this task is about doing something at the same time every day, no matter, as well

as spreading a little positive energy into the world. You can do it at 9am, 11am or 1pm, but it must be the same time every day.

"As soon as you trust yourself, you will know how to live."

-Johann Wolfgang von Goethe

Chapter Seven:

I Love It When a Plan Comes Together

Now, it's time to start putting the pieces together and to learn how to create incredible dates that allow the opportunity for you and your partner to create memories, polar energy and trust. If we start methodically, planning a great date is like planning a business. First we decide what our desired outcome is and from this point, we can work out all of the details.

I'll give you an example of a date that I went on with a radiant woman. It was my goal to convey to her how incredible I thought she was and create a situation where I could relish her beauty and her femininity. I decided on a classic "restaurant date," where we would both enjoy some delectable food and where we would be without any distractions, televisions or cell phones. I really wanted to stare into her eyes and tell her some of things that had been sitting in my heart.

I didn't tell her what we were going to be doing that Thursday night, or where we would be going. I simply arranged a date with her earlier in the week so that she would know I was up to something. I informed her that I would be sending further instructions via email that would give her all of the details she needed before the date. In the email I stated the pick-up time, that we would be eating and that she should dress in something *classically sexy*. I could have just asked her to dress for a formal evening, but what fun would that be?

Thursday arrived and in the morning I sent her a text message. "I cannot wait to have you in my arms in a few hours. We are going to have an incredible night." I got an instant reply telling me that she was very excited to see what we were going to be doing. I arrived about five minutes early and rang the bell. I was wearing a crispy white pressed shirt with an open collar, cuff links, pressed dress pants and polished shoes. I was wearing her favorite cologne. She opened the door and was wearing... her bathrobe. I stepped inside and put my hands on her face and gave her a deep kiss that must have weakened her knees judging by her swoon.

She apologized for not being ready and ran off to the bathroom to finish up whatever it is she needed do before a date. I told her we had lots of time as we were only about 15 minutes away from our destination and we didn't need to leave for another 20 minutes or so. I could see her body posture instantly change as she realized that she didn't have to rush and that she wasn't holding us up.

I went into the living room and read a magazine until she was ready. When she made her appearance, I was speechless. She was an incredible sight of beauty and pure white energy. With my mouth still wide open, I managed to get out the words, "You look absolutely angelic!" I just stood there and allowed my eyes to completely take in her radiance.

I handed her a sealed envelope that was obviously a card. I asked her to not open the envelope but leave it on the table until later. I explained that I had been working on my psychic abilities and that everything would make sense when the card was read later. At this point in our relationship she had just come to accept that I always was up to something. She also knew that it usually worked out in her favor, so she did as I asked and placed the card aside and we left.

As we walked up to the car, I opened her door and offered my hand to assist her into the seat. In the car two bottles of water were sitting in the drink holder, just in case we wanted it. Of course the car was immaculately clean. I had made a CD for my car that had a few songs that had some meaning to us. The music started to play as soon as I turned on the engine and it only took the first few bars before I saw a little smile playing on her lips and knew the music was entirely on target.

At this point, she still had no idea where we were going or what we were doing, so we started to play a little game where she guessed a new destination with every turn we made. In a conversation we had a few weeks earlier, she was telling me about her parents courtship and how her Dad used to take her mother to a little waterfront restaurant. I had arranged for us to dine at the same restaurant. I thought it was a romantic idea and so did she. It was renowned for its amazing food and a setting with beautiful views of the harbor.

As we walked into the restaurant, we were greeted by the maitre d' and I gave him my name. I had requested a table where we could enjoy the evening view. As we walked towards our table, I waited until she decided which seat she would like at the table, helped with her jacket, then helped her into her chair. Once she was settled, I sat down, reached across the table, took her hand in mine and kissed it.

I perused the wine list and asked her if she had any preference or if she would like me to make a selection. She asked me to choose. Realizing that we were at a seafood place and looking at the wines with some sort of familiarity, I chose a nice well rounded red Italian, Masi Valpolicella, I had enjoyed before. Table wines like the Masi are usually full of flavor but don't linger too long in your mouth. It would complement almost any food dish that we ordered, without overpower it.

She told me she had narrowed the menu down to two entrees. I answered, "I was thinking about those as well. Why don't I order 'X' and you order 'Y' and we can have some of each." A perfect solution to get everything we wanted. I ordered mains for the both of us and included a small appetizer that I knew she would enjoy sharing with me and a bottle of sparkling water to be served with dinner.

Dinner was amazing and we laughed and talked about everything you could imagine. From our favorite cartoon characters when we were kids to where we would like to travel in the next few years. The dessert menu came and I suggested that we order one dessert and share it. I asked for two forks.

Halfway through our dessert, the bill was delivered and I took it and placed my credit card on top. She offered to pay for her half. I explained the date was my pleasure and said if she would like to take me on another date sometime, I would be open to such a gesture.

After we finished our meals, I assisted her out of her chair and helped her put on her jacket. We walked arm in arm back to the car where I opened the door and offered my hand to help her into the seat. As we started driving, I let her know that there was one more stop before home. She wanted to know right away what it was, but I just asked her to trust me. Creating suspense for a few minutes can be very exciting for both of you.

A few weeks earlier we were on a walk and she told me about a list she had been working on of different places in world that she would like to be kissed. One of the places was a gazebo located in a little park nearby, so this was where the next stop of the evening was going to be. As we pulled up to the closet point that I could reach in the car, I think she was still a little confused. As we exited the car, I said, "I want you to know that I love your idea about great places you want to be kissed. It's my intention to kiss you at every one of them. Let's keep adding to this list so we never run out." With that I took her hand and lead her to the gazebo, where I grabbed her in my arms and gave her one of those kisses. It was the kind of kiss that you would see at the end of an epic movie, when the couple finally reunites. The one that seems like an eternity until your lips meet, but when they do, you feel the kiss resonating deeply into your soul.

I am not one to kiss and tell but I was a little late for work the next morning. I got up and got ready quickly while my princess still lay fast asleep. I brought her the sealed envelope from the night before and laid it upon the pillow next to her. Right before I left, I whispered in her ear to not forget to open the envelope when she awoke.

You must be wondering exactly what I put on my card.

> *My dearest angel,*
>
> *It was both a great honor and pleasure to be able to hold you in my eyes last night for so many hours. You are the woman that I choose every day in my life. You are my first thought each morning and the last thought before I close my eyes each evening. I thank you for the way you bring smiles into my life. The kiss that we shared last night I am sure will be one of our top 10 kisses for all time. I cannot wait to find you in my arms again.*
>
> *Love James.*

I received a text message later that morning asking that I make an effort to come to her house for lunch that day. There was some mention about a cowboy hat and red high heels...

This is a great example of a well-planned and well-executed date. If you examine the date and look for examples of the true ability to shine as a gentleman, you will see many of the lessons from Sir John McCallum.

Patience: In being accommodating when I first arrived for the date and just allowing her the time she needed to get ready.

Being on purpose: I had a definite plan for the evening. I had a goal and knew how I could achieve it.

Going First Class: Ordering a bottle of wine, having sparkling water with dinner.

Dress with purpose: Looking the part with polished shoes, cuff links and pressed clothes.

Scents make sense: I made sure I was wearing great cologne that I knew she would appreciate.

Time is a virtue: I was appropriately early for our arranged meeting time.

Never let them see you sweat: I had pre-arranged a little flexibility around our pick-up time. If she had been ready on time, I planned to drive around a beautiful park near the restaurant. As it turned out, she never needed to know about this part of the evening and it was never missed.

Choose your reaction: With the right plans in place, I was able to stay joyful even when part of the night had to be cancelled due to the young lady not being ready on time.

Chivalry is alive and well: Every door opened every time. Hand out to assist into car. Walking arm and arm to and from restaurant, doing the "Pretty Woman" move when she stands up from a table you do the half stand up , pushing in her chair at the restaurant, helping her with her jacket, ordering our dinners.

ABC –Always be clean: my car was freshly cleaned and well prepared for the evening with water and music. I was freshly cleaned too!

Keeping your eyes on the target: There was no doubt the only woman I saw that evening was the woman of my dreams across from me. I knew it and so did she.

All of these choices allow a date to see the quality of man that you are. These all go back to developing the trust between a woman and a man and how that advances your relationship. The lessons that we learned from Sir John McCallum are invaluable. You already know these rules, but do you practice them? What is the cost if we do not? What is the ROI (return on investment) if you do?

Be the exceptional man that you know how to be. Take the time to practice and learn anything you need to in order to become that exceptional man. It is the only way to truly have the woman of your dreams to be fully and completely committed to building a life with and satisfying you at the deepest levels.

CHALLENGE SEVEN

Recall the dates that you have planned in the past, that in your mind, have been your most successful. The dates that you know the love of your life would regard as some of your greatest moments. Imagine you are making a highlight reel of your courtship best moves ever, list the top five.

1. _____

2. _____

3. _____

4. _____

5. _____

Chapter Eight:

Steps to Conjuring Magic

*"It is important to remember that
we all have **magic** inside us."*

J.K. Rowling

We have identified many actions that can give your romance an opportunity to grow. But how do you set up the actual event? What do you need to consider before you can shine as a truly great man? Let's break it down into a workable structure:

Goal – What memory do I hope to create on this date?

Time – What can I give and what can I ask her to give?

Cost — How much do I want to spend to make this all happen?

Preferences — What would we enjoy doing together?

Dating Foreplay – How can I build the excitement before the date even happens?

First Impression — What can I do to start off the date on the right foot?

Flexibility — How can I be prepared for anything that comes up?

Shining Man Moment — What will she remember when the date is over?

Sweet Goodnight— How am I going to bring this date to a perfect close?

Post-Game Show — What can I do to reinforce the memories we created together?

Goal

Before you start planning a great date, it's important to understand what you are trying to achieve. This may sound a little mechanical to some; however, without clear vision it is difficult to achieve great success in anything. When it comes to investing in the love of my life, I take very few chances. I look at the type of energy I want to create or what memory I want to add into our lives. Sometimes I may want to create a date that allows us to have tremendous fun together. Sometimes it may be to create a romantic situation and reveal how I feel about her. Other times it may be about creating a situation where we need to work together on a project, or possibly challenge ourselves either physically or mentally, both which in turn could be considered a form of growth together. Some dates may involve making her feel completely spoiled or taking care of her at a level that she rarely treats herself to. Some dates could be about being put into social group dynamic settings and sometimes the date could be about showing your partner a side of you that perhaps they don't know yet. When we look at the ultimate goal of any date it is easy to recognize that we are trying to create a situation where we are seen in a positive light so that the person we are spending time with wants to be in our future and wants to spend more time with us. We want to create a state of bliss for that person. We want that person's feelings to grow and have ours grow alongside them.

If we look at the date I highlighted earlier, it was very clear that I had a specific goal. I wanted to create time and space for me to appreciate and adore the woman of my dreams.

Time

How much time do we really need for a great date? I don't think that there is a right answer. A well planned date could be as short as 10 minutes or as long as a week or more. It is about creating a plan that is sensitive to both of your schedules. Before we start to come up with great ideas to spend time together it's necessary to address this detail. Whatever the answer is, it's just part of the planning, not an excuse to cut corners or miss the opportunity all together. Sacrificing other areas of your lives to be together can be very dangerous. Don't ask the woman that you adore to change too much, she may change into someone that you are not as passionate about! Honor the time that you both have and find a way to play within it.

In my perfect date, outlined in the last chapter, I arranged early on that a whole evening would be acceptable. It gave me time to make sure that I had my life all taken care of and that I could afford the time. This way when we arrived at the day, we were both ready to fully commit our attentions to one another.

Cost

Heaven forbid that people should ever talk about money. What a load of crap. Dating can be expensive if you're not made of money. You can't and shouldn't try to continually *buy* memories with your woman. Before I plan a date I definitely consider what the pattern has been in our last few dates. Have we been out to some nice places? Have we been doing things on the cheap? I believe that a balance is important. If you went out to incredibly high-end restaurants *all* of the time, they would no longer be considered a treat–they would become the norm. Anything in excess seems imbalanced. Well, except maybe sex. But even then it has to be a little different all the time or it just becomes routine. Sometimes I plan dates that cost absolutely nothing and other times I choose not to worry about what my credit card statement will look like at the end of the month. If I include this step in my planning, it keeps the creativity efforts up. Spending a little money is more difficult than spending a lot. Making those efforts that come at no expense are often more appreciated than ones that someone else creates and you pay for. If you are looking to save a little money when you are going out on the town, investigate The Entertainment Book, it is available in most major cities in North America.

Be content to pay whatever you need to, but go to a restaurant you can afford. The second part of the date, the kiss in the gazebo, cost absolutely nothing. For me it was that part of the evening that will always be remembered. I cannot recall the precise taste of the bottle of wine we had or the exact flavors of the dishes we ordered, but every time we pass that gazebo, we both have smiles on our faces.

Preferences

If you were going out with a best friend, you would want to do something that the both of you would enjoy. That is the essence of hanging out with a friend. The woman in your life should be one of your best friends. I really enjoy country music. The love of my life doesn't like country one iota. There is no point in me planning a date for us to go and see Garth Brooks. You need to find activities that you can both participate in at the same level. I know when it comes to sports that this can be a difficult task. My partner is an amazing skier, so we can enjoy that together. However, if one of us was considerably better than the other, it would require one of us to play at a level that was less than we normally would. Eventually this could lead to some undue stress.

Choose activities you both love. Find the places where you have a lot in common with your woman. Play together in those areas. Don't think that you need to do everything together. Keep your own interests and have some incredible male friends that you can go out and "date" for those other activities. I know I just implied you should "date" your friends and I mean it. Why wouldn't you put forth the same effort for your mates as you would for your mate?

Dating Foreplay

This ties in directly with courtship. Anything you do before the date that get a woman excited about the event before it even happens is dating foreplay. You can arrange the time of the date with her but play a game of 20 questions for her to guess where you are going. There are phone calls, text messages and notes and any number of ways to play in the romance before you actually get to the date. Mystery can play a great part of this foreplay as well. Holding back little bits of information will heighten the anticipation of the date. Be sincere in your excitement of the date and it will always come back to you. Play and have fun.

The request for the date with no real explanations of the event and asking for a little trust was the first part of building the suspense. Secondly, emailing the details with the *ambiguous* dress request drew many questions. Finally, there was the great phone message I left the day of the date. She commented on it later that night, saying that she was pleased to hear the excitement in my voice regarding that night.

First Impression

Don't show up empty-handed to a date. Always bring something as a gift or to use on the date itself. This may include two boxed and wrapped wine glasses that you intend to use at the beach with a bottle of wine. Every time she uses these glasses, she will have a great memory attached to them and you will keep her in a state of "recall bliss." Recall bliss happens when you attach amazing memories to objects or places you keep seeing or using. Let's say you are going out for a fancy French dinner so maybe you get a little Eiffel Tower fridge magnet. Wrap it in paper and give it to your lover at the beginning of the evening but explain that she cannot open it until you get back home.

After the date when she opens it just simply say that you bought this to help her remember the incredible night you knew you would have together. Now every time she opens the fridge and sees this— recall bliss. The small gift at the beginning is an easy way to start off on the right foot. Mix it up often. Have fun with it. It's easy to add in a little mystery to heighten the experience.

In my dinner date example the first impression was simply the envelope. It was a little pre-planning that set up the whole night. The card within the envelope became the recall bliss every time she saw it. It now lives in our scrapbook and when we look back, the memories of how we fell in love are crystal clear again. The little things totally count.

Flexibility

Every date needs to have a little flexibility in it. You need to be flexible in your departure times, you need a backup plan in case things go sideways, you need to keep your cool and think on your feet if need be. When you are arranging a departure time, assume that she will not be ready. That way you are never disappointed. As we spoke about in the lessons from Sir John McCallum, there are strategies you can apply in this situation, like the pre-date little stop for coffee.

If you cannot be flexible with time, make sure that you make this very clear to your date before the day of the event. Be kind and remind her the day of as back up. Having a backup plan takes all of the stress out of the date for you. I once chose a restaurant that my date absolutely refused to go to because she had got food poisoning the last time she was there. How was I to know??? Because I had a backup plan, there was another restaurant already selected in the neighbourhood just in case the wait was going to be too long at my first choice. Thank God I had the second location.

There are some times when you need to be quick on your feet. Don't get so attached to a date idea that you overlook the fact that the goal is to spend time with your date. Another time, I had planned a picnic date. We had just set up the blanket when the weather started to change. By the time the meal was out of the basket, it was raining. My backup plan was to use the picnic shelter that was just a couple minutes walk away. But the wind was picking up to and it was clearly no longer an outside sort of day. I packed up everything and asked if she would mind if we did something completely bizarre. She agreed.

I drove us to the mall where I knew that there was a bench near a little fountain. It was a great date. With the depth of conversation that we held, the world soon disappeared. We sat on that bench for over four hours enjoying each other's company. I even got us a couple of hot coffees from the little cafe a couple of shops down. The date was even better than I could have ever planned because I stayed flexible.

Shining Man Moment

The sign of any great date is how quickly afterwards there are updates being sent to girlfriends of the woman that you dated. Shining man moments are often the first thing she wants to tell everyone about. They are also the moments that will become memories as the years go by. They are moments of you being a truly great man. They are the moments that separate you from every other man she has ever known. You have the opportunity to *create* these moments as well as be *aware* of the magical moments that just simply appear. Shining man moments also often fall into the category of courtship.

These little efforts that we make outside our normal lives can fill the heart of our woman even when we are not around. They give you massive mileage. You can do something once and it will forever be attached to your woman's opinion of who you are. Remember the story of me making a dinner for my mother, the shining man moment was the act of preparing and cooking for her. She usually was the one who had always cooked for us. The fact that I took that on for her gave her the belief that I will be a great cook. She always looks forward to occasions when I cook for her. When I do this, she always sees it as a sign of my love for her.

With my date example, the setting up of the kiss in the park was a glaring shining man moment. This allowed her to do something that had been on her list and added one more romantic moment. It was clearly a highlight of the night and the part that we will talk about for many years to come.

Sweet Goodnight

One of the biggest missed opportunities that I regularly hear about from couples is the end of the date. Have you ever had an incredible night out and then come home and go back to your routine. You get home and go your separate ways; doing those "very important" pre-bed checklists that you both have. What a missed opportunity!

A great date has this final stage already pre-planned. Let us infer that you were planning a massage when you got home that night. You of course would have purchased some new oil for later that night and given it as a little gift at the beginning of the date; wrapped and with instructions not to open until later. At some point in the evening you can sow the seeds and let her know that when you get home you would love more than anything to slowly remove all of her clothes, lay her on the bed and allow your hands to caress and massage every inch of her body until she reaches a true state of euphoria. Trust me, this will work and you will forever be a *good night* planner.

In the example above, I had the intention to bring the music in the car into the house at the end of the night. I was planning to hold her in my arms and dance with her on the deck with the stars above us. It would have been a great end to the night and further set up the chance at romance. It didn't happen but it was still one of the most passionate nights of my life.

Post-Game Show

Anchoring memories is a truly masterful technique that will always serve you well. We all take photos as a way of capturing memories and this can work exceptionally on dates. One thing that I do with my partner is keep all the wine corks from those special days we want to remember. One of us takes 20 seconds to write a few words on the cork itself and then we throw it into a jar in the kitchen—it's recall bliss every time we go in the kitchen where the corks are. Hang on to ticket stubs and start a small box for you to keep them in can be a great little gift. We have everything from concert tickets to a speeding ticket in our box. Picking up a rock or a shell or a leaf from some adventure that you had outside may serve as a perfect reminder. Collect matchbooks from restaurants or hotels you've visited and make an international collection. Find ways that work for you. I even started a journal for the amazing dates that we have, so we can look back and re-live the experience. I write details of the night down and ask for the little details my partner remembers, so she can then instantly recall them later that week. Learning what makes you partner's heart tick can be used in future date planning, no point in reinventing the wheel when all the answers are sitting right in front of you.

With my date, the card and the music we played is my post-game show. These actions were well planned with multiple purposes and remain very effective.

Is it all worth it? I would never give something as important as the success of my relationship with any less care. Putting forth a little time and creativity to make sure every date becomes a great memory for both you and your sweetheart is one of the keys to true relationship success. I dare you to try some planning and see how your woman responds. Become a whiz at creating these incredible dates and I promise you will reap the benefits.

CHALLENGE EIGHT

Plan an incredible date. You have 90 minutes with the love of your life on a Monday night from 7:30 pm to 9:00 pm. The rest is up to you. Simply work through the work sheet on the next page.

DATE WORK SHEET

Goal—What memory do I hope to create on this date?

_____

_____

Time—What can I give and what can I ask of her to give?

_____

_____

Cost—How much do I want to spend to make this all happen?

_____

_____

Preferences—What would we enjoy doing together?

_____

_____

Dating Foreplay—How can I build the excitement before the date?

_____

_____

First Impression—What can I do to start off the date on the right foot ?

_____

_____

Flexibility—How can I be prepared for anything that comes up?

_____

_____

Shining Man Moment—What will she remember when the date is over?

_____

_____

Sweet Goodnight—How am I going to bring this date to a perfect close?

_____

_____

Post-Game Show—What can I do to reinforce the memories we created together?

_____

_____

Chapter Nine:
Now What???

I wouldn't dare leave you, who have invested the time to read this book, without a simple executable plan to complete. I challenge you to faithfully follow the Courtship Calendar (found in the back of this book and online) for the next 30 days and see how your relationship transforms. This tool makes your life simpler and helps you fully engage the heart of your woman.

It provides the framework for success and suggestions on how often you should date the love of your life. It provides ideas regarding all of the little things you should be doing that inspire the process of courtship. The calendar gives you a plan for the first month and it's designed to take your relationship to a new level.

For each day on the calendar that has actions listed on it, there will also be detailed suggestions on how to achieve the simple tasks. The version that I created online is more comprehensive and along with many other tips and tools for your success, available via my website, www.GetYourWifeInBed.com . For this first month I've included a hard copy found at the back of this book to get you started immediately or you can go online and download a free PDF version to print or a version that will sync with your computer's personal organizer.

Keep as close to this schedule as you can. If you need to modify the days, simply try to keep all activities in the same week. If you run into the challenge of not being in same the city at the same time, modify the dating portions, where possible, to be phone dates or webcam dates. Ensure you phrase your request delicately here. Any misunderstanding regarding a "webcam date" could result in unnecessary drama! The possibilities are endless and are only limited by your imagination.

Let's look at the first month's events. Below you will find an expanded version of each of the tasks throughout the calendar. Refer to the Courtship Calendar at the end of the book to get all the dates to execute the following.

Week One

Send a letter. Do not skip this step! It's important. This letter is designed to let the woman of your dreams know you intend to work on your relationship. This way she is not taken aback when you start initiating all of these new ideas around dating and courtship. You want her to know that you are investing into the two of you as a couple. Here is an example letter to work from. Use the template but modify it so it becomes your words and has your story.

> *To my love,*
>
> *I remember the first time I ever kissed you like it was yesterday. (Insert your story) When we started our relationship I was fully committed to proving to you that I was a man worthy of your heart and your hand. I would like to put you on notice that I am committing to winning your heart every day. I will be trying some new and old ideas to ignite the passion between us. Please be patient with me as*

*I strive to succeed beyond either of our wildest dreams in
this endeavor. It's my intent to create time and space for us
to grow together. I look forward to feeling enchanted with
one another once again.*

With all of my heart,

(Put your name or your special name that she calls you)

I would encourage you to go and buy a nice piece of paper from a
stationary store and handwrite this letter. Send via snail mail. It is
amazing how few pieces of mail we receive that are a joy to open
and read. It is the first little gift to your lady and should reflect
the amount of detail and attention you intend to put into your
relationship. You need to get it into the mail Monday morning
so that it will get to her by Wednesday.

Execute the First Short Date. This is designed as a small sample
of the thoughtful randomness that is about to fall into the life of
your angel. But, this is an impromptu date. It can be as simple
as a candlelit dinner at home or a walk topped off with a bottle
of wine. How about a 30-minute sunrise date? Creativity wins
women's hearts. If you are struggling for ideas, sign up for free
online to the *member only area* to gain access to the DATERIX.
This tool is a powerful search engine that will allow you to input
specify date criteria and be given ample ideas to either be used
or to spark your genius. The goal of this first date is to isolate a
short amount of time and space for you to start to reconnect.
Take time from your busy normal day and just give her your
undivided attention. Break whatever patterns you have had in
the past, do something a little different and call it a date.

Leave a Thank You Note. Put it somewhere she is going to find
it. On her pillow, on the counter in the bathroom, in her car or

in her bag, find a location that she will absolutely see the note. In the note, simply thank her for her time on your first date. Tell her what you enjoyed about your time together and then close with how much you look forward to seeing her at the end of the day.

Week Two

Give Her a Before-Work Massage. This is a great setup for the week. On Monday morning, I want you to set your alarm 15 minutes earlier than usual. When it goes off, explain that you set your alarm early so you would have time to give your lady a short massage before you start your day and week. Ask her to allow herself to be totally pampered by you for 15 minutes.

Ask Her On a Date for Saturday. This is where you create some mystery around what is coming this weekend. Getting this commitment early in the week will allow the excitement to build and to ensure an amazing evening. It also leaves her enough room to arrange her schedule. Don't give any real date details away at this point. Just get the commitment.

Plan the Date. Use all the techniques laid out for you in Chapter Seven. Choose something you know she will love and don't miss any of the steps.

Send an Email Regarding Date Info. Send a simple email outlining the bare necessities: departure time, what to wear, any special details, whether food will be involved and when. Remember, this is not one of your business contacts or meeting the guys for hockey. You're not, "Going to grab a burger or something." The way you phrase the email can make a big difference to her anticipation. "We will be dining at 8" may help you out. This little bit of information will allow your date to be ready and prepared for you and your evening.

Have a Great Date. This is what you have been planning. DON'T over think it. If everything goes perfectly according to plan, great. If nothing in your plan works like you thought, great. The whole idea behind this date was to have some time with your goddess and you have achieved that. Have fun together and enjoy the experience. Be mindful of the lessons Sir McCallum has taught us.

An Early Morning Big Kiss and Thank You. At a random time during the morning just lay one on her. Dip her over if it is appropriate. Thank her for an amazing time last night. Then just walk away. This is not a prelude to more intimate contact. It is just a thank you... and a great kiss.

Week Three

Phone Call to Incite Recall Bliss of the Date. Either get a hold of her on the phone or leave a voice message highlighting your favorite part of the date two days ago. She will most likely reply with her best memory as well. This anchors the memories for both of you. It reinforces the fun that you had together.

Get a Random Gift. Find a little something that you can give to your sweetheart. It should be small in price and big in thought. It could be a book that she has wanted to read. It could be some coupons that you create for some services you would like to offer to her for example "Good for One Coffee Date" or "Redeem for a Two-Minute Kiss." The gift could be a mixed CD you make her for her car. Be creative and make sure to wrap it up and give it to her. We all love to unwrap presents.

*Do your best to recall what *types* of gifts usually affect her the most. There are tools on the website to help with this. Does she enjoy the little kisses more than your offer to have her car washed? Do your little notes or cards with special words of appreciation leave that expression on her face more than a new bottle of aromatherapy bath salts? Does she still stress about getting all the kids to activities on time? How about offering to drive them to school or hockey practice for a day to surprise her? As you decode your woman's language you'll enjoy easy success truly knowing how to speaking to her heart.

Sign up for my Courtship Calendar.
Visit www.GetYourWifeInBed.com and you can receive next month's calendar to capitalize on the momentum you've started. As her heart softens and she sinks more into her feminine energy she will trust you more and more and you'll see greater success from your efforts building upon each other. When you **sign up online** as a member, simple take a few extra minutes and fill in a DATE WORK SHEET with your best date idea and you will receive your second month of the Courtship Calendar **absolutely FREE**. The second month's calendar will appear in your email box within days.

Afternoon Activity Date with Photo Shoot. Plan to do something outside if possible. Anytime we reconnect with nature, we feel energized and de-stressed. Associating those feeling with one another is brilliant. Take a camera with you and get some photos of you playing together or holding each other. Create those memories. Good ideas could be hiking, walking on the beach, sports, a picnic, making a snowman, having a rubber ducky race, or even going to a park that you always just drive by.

Week Four

Give Framed Photo from a Photo Shoot. Look at all the photos you took the other day and find one or two that show you both having fun together or being connected somehow. If you are stuck picking a good picture, ask someone for help. But pick a good one, because it will remind you both of the reasons you fell in love and of the future joy you can share.

Ask For a Late Night Date. We want to continue to break our old patterns. By asking for a date that will occur late in the evening tomorrow, it adds a little mystery again and makes your woman curious about what you are up to. Make the date for around 11pm, or whatever time is late in her schedule.

Candlelight Dessert. Plan to have an exquisite dessert. Make it yourself or pick something up from the store. Ask her not to enter a pre-decided part of the house while you prepare for the date. Light as many candles as it takes to give the room a warm glow. You can pick up huge bags of tea lights at many stores. Lay out the dessert and champagne for the two of you. Go and get her and ask her to close her eyes (or use a silk scarf if you have one) as you lead her to the date. This is great because it builds trust and adds that last little bit of mystery. When you arrive, ask her to uncover her eyes and enjoy the evening. Don't be too surprised if things turn physical.

Write a Poem. This may be hard, but you need to try. Your effort will be appreciated. Men don't often take time to make this old-world gesture. Write from your heart; don't worry about forming real sentences. Take the time to handwrite it. When you go to present it, read it out loud to her and then give her a copy. Kiss her and tell her how much you love her after the reading.

By the time you reach the four-week mark, you will be amazed at where you have arrived in your relationship. The woman in your life will trust that you are serious about capturing her heart every day. She will be looking forward to your next date. She will be dressing a little differently to get your attention. You will be connecting on a different level to how you did just 30 days earlier. Imagine what your life will be like when she always receives this level of engagement from you. If you don't have your wife back in bed yet, it won't be long. To continue your current results and keep growing from this point simply: **Keep going....more dates and more courtship.**

Visit the website immediately to sign up for the Courtship Calendar, get tons of free dating ideas and register for our many contests. www.GetYourWifeInBed.com

Chapter Ten:

The Man's Quick Review Chapter

Review this if you start to forget what you've learned.

The Basic Concept: Continually date the woman of your dreams and you will always have the same or more success than you had in the beginning of the relationship.

Believe You Can Make the Difference: There is no point trying to blame anything or anyone because your relationship has changed over time. If you are not getting what you want from it; this is your opportunity to lead and make the necessary changes to get the results you both want.

Know What Women Want: A man that is *present* and *on purpose*.

Challenge Yourself to Be Better: Look through the lessons from Sir John McCallum and address any areas that you can improve upon. Everyone needs ongoing attention to all of these areas. Start with learning how to deflect your eyes. It will be a real eye opener.

Understand How Love Grows: A woman's heart is captured and her love ignited by allowing her to find ways to trust you and create unforgettable memories together. Dating helps you achieve these goals with ease and grace. It takes time, but it will entirely transform you both.

Learn to be a Whiz: Understand and practice the art of creating masterful dates. Use all of the points discussed in these pages and tools on the website and apply them. Put the magic back into your lives.

Use the Tools: Take advantage of the FREE Courtship Calendar at the back of this book or log onto www.GetYourWifeinBed.com and download a free version of the Calendar that will sync onto your personal organiser. You will also have access to video blogs that teaches and expands upon Sir John McCallum's lessons. It's free. Signing up online as a member will get you access to the DATERIX, a search engine that will provide you with dating ideas based on certain criteria. It's easy to use, fun and fast. Allow yourself to be in the relationship that you have always wanted with your true love. We don't need to reinvent the wheel, or struggle to come up with new ideas, we just need to share some knowledge and apply it.

CAUTION***

There might be thousands of reason that you will not start this program right away. I've heard them all. You need to ask yourself:

What is more important than making **myself** and **my Goddess** happy?

- I can tell you it isn't your kids. Without your relationship as strong as possible, they won't learn the lessons that will shape their lives. If you are having a challenge getting time alone with your significant other, why not date the whole family. You are a creative man and can make anything happen.

- It isn't work, if you believe that money is the answer to your relationship happiness, you are sadly mistaken. I am not saying that money isn't important, but there are a lot of men who are both wealthy and unhappy.

- It isn't TV or the internet or what you do in your free time.

Your relationship is your most valued asset. It must continually grow in order to survive. Start today and **invest in your entire life**. You will become the wealthiest and happiest man you know. You have a plan. You have a purpose. Go and play. Love you life and everyone in it.

I challenge you to follow this courting schedule with your sweetheart for the next four weeks. It is designed as a simple reminder of what we can do to truly appreciate our women. Please take notice of the changes to your relationship by the end of this period. You can share your successful results online at www.GetYourWifeInBed.com.

(See accompanying notes in NOW WHAT? Chapter for full explanation of all tasks)

FIRST MONTH COURTSHIP CALENDAR

Week 4	Week 3	Week 2	Week 1	
	Telephone call memory recall for date	Before work massage	Send letter	M
		Ask out for date on Saturday		T
Give framed picture from shoot		Plan Saturday's Date		W
Ask for late night date Friday	Little Random Gift	Send email regarding date info	Execute quick short date	T
Candlelight Dessert	SIGNUP for Courtship Calendar		Leave note thanking for date	F
		Have a great date		S
Write her a poem	Afternoon activity date photo shoot		Early morning big kiss and thank for date	S

BUY A SHARE OF THE FUTURE IN YOUR COMMUNITY

These certificates make great holiday, graduation and birthday gifts that can be personalized with the recipient's name. The cost of one S.H.A.R.E. or one square foot is $54.17. The personalized certificate is suitable for framing and will state the number of shares purchased and the amount of each share, as well as the recipient's name. The home that you participate in "building" will last for many years and will continue to grow in value.

Here is a sample SHARE certificate:

THIS CERTIFIES THAT

YOUR NAME HERE
HAS INVESTED IN A HOME FOR A DESERVING FAMILY

1985-2005

TWENTY YEARS OF BUILDING FUTURES IN OUR COMMUNITY ONE HOME AT A TIME

1200 SQUARE FOOT HOUSE @ $65,000 = $54.17 PER SQUARE FOOT
This certificate represents a tax deductible donation. It has no cash value.

YES, I WOULD LIKE TO HELP!

I support the work that Habitat for Humanity does and I want to be part of the excitement! As a donor, I will receive periodic updates on your construction activities but, more importantly, I know my gift will help a family in our community realize the dream of homeownership. **I would like to SHARE in your efforts against substandard housing in my community!** *(Please print below)*

PLEASE SEND ME _____ SHARES at $54.17 EACH = $ $_____

In Honor Of: _____

Occasion: (Circle One)   HOLIDAY   BIRTHDAY   ANNIVERSARY

      OTHER: _____

Address of Recipient: _____

Gift From: _____ *Donor Address:* _____

Donor Email: _____

I AM ENCLOSING A CHECK FOR $ $_____ PAYABLE TO HABITAT FOR HUMANITY OR PLEASE CHARGE MY VISA OR MASTERCARD *(CIRCLE ONE)*

Card Number _____ Expiration Date: _____

Name as it appears on Credit Card _____ Charge Amount $ _____

Signature _____

Billing Address _____

Telephone # Day _____ Eve _____

PLEASE NOTE: Your contribution is tax-deductible to the fullest extent allowed by law.
Habitat for Humanity • P.O. Box 1443 • Newport News, VA 23601 • 757-596-5553
www.HelpHabitatforHumanity.org

Printed in the USA
CPSIA information can be obtained
at www.ICGtesting.com
JSHW082221140824
68134JS00015B/661